IMAGES
of America

HASTINGS

FLORIDA'S POTATO CAPITAL

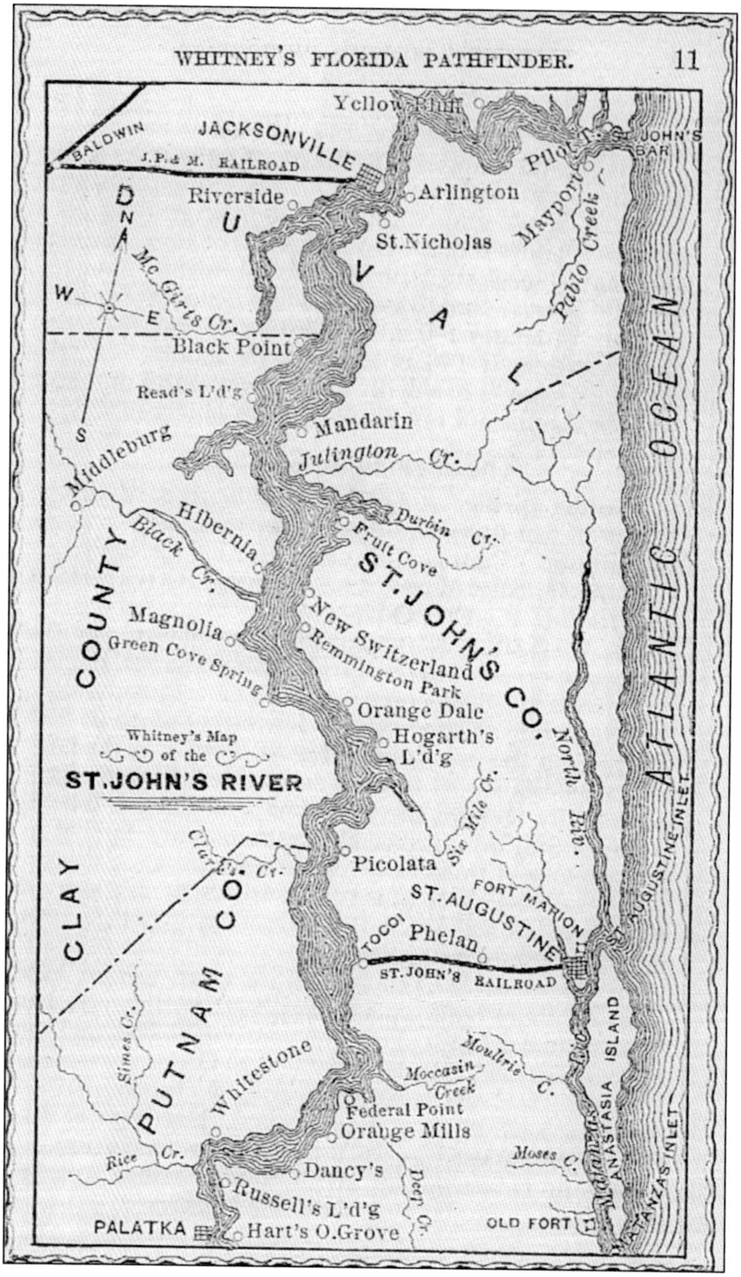

John Prescott Whitney began publishing *Whitney's Florida Pathfinder* soon after the end of the Civil War. His popular tourist guide was published in New York City and targeted those who were wealthy enough to winter in warmer climates. This map of the St. Johns River appeared in *Whitney's Florida Pathfinder* in 1876. (Courtesy of the author.)

ON THE COVER: A team of workers is shown in 1947 at a Hastings potato-grading facility filling a truck with baskets and bags of Hastings potatoes. Soon, the load of potatoes would be taken to the Florida East Coast (FEC) Railway depot and transferred to boxcars for shipment to markets all over the United States. (Florida Memory.)

IMAGES
of America

HASTINGS

FLORIDA'S POTATO CAPITAL

Gregory Leonard

ARCADIA
PUBLISHING

ISBN 978-1-4671-0642-9

Published by Arcadia Publishing
Charleston, South Carolina

Printed in the United States of America

Library of Congress Control Number: 2020949642

For all general information, please contact Arcadia Publishing:
Telephone 843-853-2070
Fax 843-853-0044
E-mail sales@arcadiapublishing.com
For customer service and orders:
Toll-Free 1-888-313-2665

Visit us on the Internet at www.arcadiapublishing.com

This book is dedicated to the memory of Frances McElveen Parish, who, for 28 years, wrote a daily column for the St. Augustine Record *featuring the news from Hastings. Frances was considered the historian for Southwestern St. Johns and Eastern Putnam Counties. Her personal archives, passed on to her daughter Nancy Parish Towns, were essential to the creation of this book.*

Contents

ACKNOWLEDGMENTS

The author wishes to thank Nancy Parish Towns, whose photographs and contributions to many of the captions in this book were invaluable and greatly appreciated. A historian in her own right, Nancy provided research and shared her personal experience of growing up in the Hastings community that was instrumental in our being able to name many of the people in these photographs. The author also wants to thank all of those who shared their family photographs. These contributors—representing some of the pioneering families of the Hastings, Federal Point, and Orange Mills areas—include Bonnie Allen, Michele West Hicks, Tracey Mobley Jozokos, Charlotte Wilke Markham, Mary Murphy, Mary Jo Beck Perry, Susie Sheller, Wayne Smith, Christopher Stanton, and Shirley Stone.

The origins of this book go back to the fall of 2005, when the author began to collaborate with a team of local volunteers to develop a presentation that would celebrate the almost forgotten history of an area of southwest St. Johns County that included the farming communities of Elkton, Hastings, Federal Point, and Orange Mills. During the course of the development of that project, over 1,400 photographs were contributed by area families. The "live" presentation resulted in reconnecting residents old and new to the rich history of Hastings and the surrounding area. Many of the individuals who contributed to that presentation have since passed on, but their stories, photographs, and—in many cases—families still remain. The contributors to the project then were William and Mary Ethel Cotton, Kenneth Deford, David Dinkins, Buzzy and Joyce DuPont, Nancy DuPont, Charles Harris, Sterling Hart, Dot Huff, Sarah Irvin, Shelby Jack, Charlotte Johns, Doug Knight, Tommy Lee, Phyllis Leonard, Dotsy Miles, Barbara Parker, Delores Pritchett, Sandy Siluvich, Wilbur Smith, Charles Stanton Jr., Tommy Tomlinson, Thelma Trent, and Freda Wilke.

Finally, the author wishes to recognize the St. Johns County Board of County Commissioners, the State Library and Archives of Florida (Florida Memory), and Bob Nawrocki and Charles Tingley of the St. Augustine Historical Society (SAHS) Research Library for their assistance, encouragement, and support during the creation of this book. The SAHS Research Library contains a tremendous collection of resources that would be of great value to anyone interested in the history of the area, the state, or the United States.

Unless otherwise noted, all photographs or postcards included in this book are from the author's collections.

Introduction

The history of Florida as we know it today is a very "new" history. The prehistory of the area began at least 4,000 years ago, when various indigenous tribes began to occupy the region. In 1947, researcher John Coggin declared that the St. Johns River Valley had "the longest history of human occupation in Florida." The original inhabitants of Northeast Florida became known as the Timucua tribes. For thousands of years, the Timucua enjoyed unrestricted access to a habitat abundant with fish and game. By 1700, those tribes had been virtually eliminated by warfare and diseases brought to the area by Europeans, but the wilderness in which they had once lived remained almost unchanged until 1900.

The story of the development of Florida, as with other areas of the United States, is about the evolution of transportation. Sailing ships and steamboats spurred the earliest development of the towns and communities along the coasts and inland along the rivers. In the 1880s, it was the rapid development of the railroads that eventually opened up access throughout the state. But it was the invention of the automobile that changed everything and provided the average American with access to the warmth and opportunity of the Sunshine State.

Our story takes place in St. Johns County, an area well-known because its county seat is St. Augustine, the "Nation's Oldest City." However, the history of St. Johns County is so rich and varied that literally every section of the county has an important story to tell.

The Hastings story begins immediately following the Civil War. Today, few can appreciate how primitive Florida was prior to the 20th century. As late as the 1870s, Florida was largely an unexplored jungle of sawgrass, swamps, Spanish bayonet, and desert-like plain. It was often described as "a place full of alligators, snakes and mosquitos."

The Town of Hastings owes its existence to Standard Oil Company cofounder Henry Flagler. In 1882, Flagler read about a land deal being put together by the State of Florida and a Philadelphia industrialist named Hamilton Disston, wherein the state sold Disston a tract of land nearly twice as large as Connecticut for 25¢ per acre. In response, Flagler decided it was time to have a look at the state that was giving away land in exchange for development.

Flagler was initially intent on building a hotel in the ancient city of St. Augustine, but his larger plan was to build hotels and create other winter destinations farther south along the east coast of Florida. Because the state was literally giving away 8,000 acres for every mile of railroad developed, Flagler decided to enter the railroad business. And it was Flagler's railroad—not his hotels—that opened up the state of Florida.

Many towns and villages developed along the Flagler railroad thanks to the efforts of small groups who established colonies at various points. In some cases, Flagler himself undertook farming on a large scale. That was the case at Hastings, where he established a model farm. In 1890, Flagler invited his cousin Thomas Horace Hastings to come to the area to raise early-harvest vegetables for the Flagler hotels. The original tract of land developed by Thomas Horace Hastings consisted of 1,569 acres on which he built greenhouses, tenant housing, and a small two-story house for his family. He named the farm Prairie Garden. Thomas Horace Hastings's first major crop appears to have been rice, but he was soon selling cucumbers, cabbage, onions, tomatoes, radishes, green peas, parsley, watercress, strawberries, and various other vegetables.

Substantial growth in the county's agricultural heritage stems from the Flagler era. Prior to that time, subsistence farming characterized the rural economy of St. Johns County. But 30 years later, Hastings and the nearby town of Elkton boasted nearly 11,000 acres that were cleared and planted with Irish potatoes alone.

By 1900, it had become widely known that big money could be made in agriculture in Florida. The mild winters gave the Hastings area an advantage over other agricultural areas of the nation, and entrepreneurs from the north and the west arrived in large numbers to seek their fortunes.

The years between 1910 and the beginning of the Great Depression in 1929 were boom times. The Gem City Improvement Company was one of the best-known promoters of what was, by then, called the "Famous Hastings Potato District." A Gem City brochure promised "large profits, a great variety of crops, no competition, independence, where potatoes 'turned to gold,' in a land of sunshine and health, with an ideal climate, combining pleasure with business."

From the perspective of the 21st century, it is difficult to appreciate just how "thriving" the Hastings community was in those years. Most of western St. Johns County was farmland, and Hastings was the hub of the entire farming region. Main Street was lined with hardware, drug, grocery, and clothing stores. Hastings even had its own newspaper—the *Hastings Herald*.

The story of Hastings and the surrounding area is the story of a town that was a center for pioneering the production of winter vegetables for cities and towns throughout the eastern United States. It is a story of rapid growth followed by the slow decline common to many farming communities in the United States. Most especially, it is a story of a group of strong, industrious, and creative people who made a lasting impact on the history of the state of Florida.

One

The Florida Wilderness

In describing the St. Johns River Valley, William Bartram said, "Blessed land where the gods have amassed into one heap all the flowering plants, birds, fish and other wildlife of two continents in order to turn the streams, the silent lake shores and the awe-abiding woodlands of this mysterious land into a true garden of Eden." Bartram, son of acclaimed English naturalist John Bartram, was an American-born botanist, ornithologist, natural historian, and explorer. William explored much of northeast Florida and the St. Johns River Valley in 1774; this was later documented in his book *Bartram's Travels*, which told of his expeditions through the southern British colonies of North America from 1773 to 1777. *The Great Florida Marsh*, painted by Martin Johnson Heade, is pictured here.

The Great Florida Sunset, shown here, was painted by Martin Johnson Heade. Heade was the first painter of national renown to make Florida his home, moving to St. Augustine in 1883. Heade traveled extensively in South America and was enthralled by the landscapes and flowers of the tropics. The tropical wilds and climate of northern Florida provided a natural environment in which Heade was able to paint until his death in 1904.

The Ocklawaha River, which flows north from central Florida for 74 miles before joining the St. Johns River, is home to abundant forms of plant, animal, reptile, and amphibious life. Of the area, William Bartram said, "We see not only flowery plants, clumps of shrubs, old weather-beaten trees with moss waving from their snags, but we also see them alive with alligators, serpents, frogs, otters, crows, herons, curlews and more."

Pioneer life in Florida was difficult. The few people who were living outside the towns and villages were typically in very primitive circumstances—often just pole shanties with hard-beaten earth floors. Many of these pioneers were educated people, including entrepreneurs who had come from cities in the North and Midwest looking for opportunities in this new frontier to the south. (Florida Memory.)

Leaving cities to come to the Florida wilderness was especially difficult for the women who accompanied men on the journey. Away from the few established population centers, there were none of the benefits of civilization. In the summer season, the heat, humidity, and swarms of mosquitos made life extremely unpleasant. (Florida Memory.)

As late as 1876, almost all of Florida's population was concentrated in the northern tier of counties bordering Georgia. Key West, the largest city in the state, had a population of about 10,000; Jacksonville had 7,000; and Tampa had less than 1,000. The principal towns along the east coast of the state between Jacksonville and Key West were St. Augustine (population 2,300) and Daytona (population 321). (Florida Memory.)

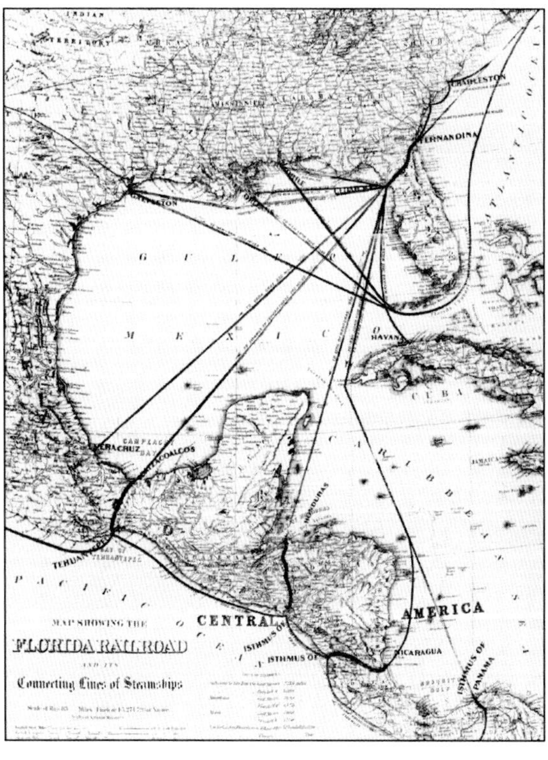

In the time of steamship travel, Key West and Cedar Key were boomtowns thanks to the steamship trade. Cedar Key was the end of the railroad line for freight coming overland in Florida, and Key West was a perfect transfer point for freight moving both north and south. Both towns were significant ports of trade with the Caribbean, Central America, and other ports within the United States.

Florida entered the golden age of steamboats following the Civil War. The first steamboat navigated the St. Johns River sandbar and inlet in 1829, and by 1851, the *Gaston*, *Magnolia*, *Ocmulgee*, *St. Matthews*, and *Welaka* were plying the waters between the port cities and along the St. Johns River. (Florida Memory.)

The steamer *City of Jacksonville* was considered one of the best steamboats on the St. Johns River and served the communities along the river for almost 40 years. Cargo and machinery were on the lower deck, passengers occupied the second deck, and the pilot's house sat on top.

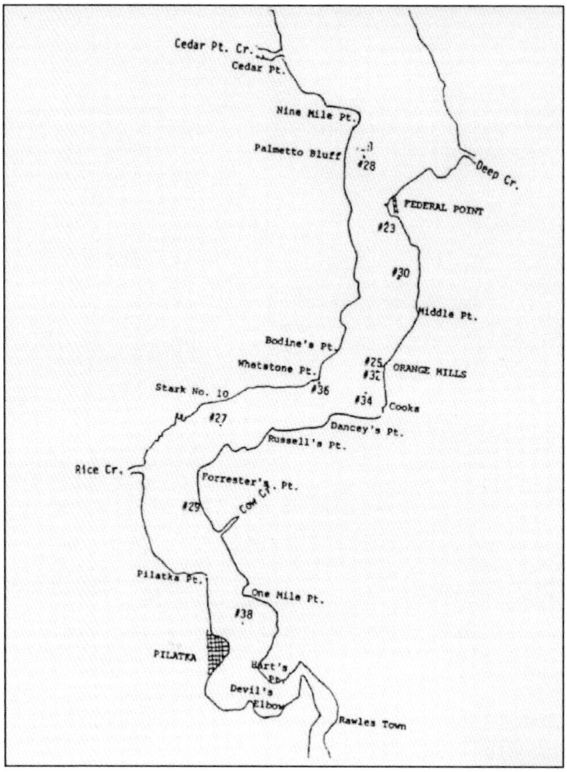

There were many small communities and landings along the St. Johns River. This c. 1870 map shows each of the communities within 20 miles of the "city" of Pilatka. Each community had its own landing from which residents could travel by steamship to Jacksonville or other communities along the river. The Federal Point landing was two miles west of what would become the town of Hastings.

John Francis Tenney, an early settler in the Federal Point area, came to Florida from New York by steamer in the winter of 1859. E. Stuart Hubbard's *Memories of Florida* states that Tenney spent his first winter in Florida making cypress shingles in a deserted logging camp. Tenney described that winter as perhaps the happiest of his life: "The creek was full of fish and the woods full of game."

John Francis Tenney left Florida at the outbreak of the Civil War and returned in 1865. The Tenney family spent that winter at Orange Mills. On one of the family's trips to Jacksonville, they noticed a white flag displayed on the banks of the river at DuPont's Landing, a location that contained just one house, which was occupied by Cornelius DuPont and family. Tenney and his brother-in-law Frank Folsom eventually purchased 1,000 acres from DuPont.

Frank Folsom and John Tenney began to develop land and build a community populated by honest and upright settlers. The land was surveyed into lots of a few acres or more and mostly sold to New Englanders who were anxious to find their places in the sun. Under Tenney's leadership, this area that was now called Federal Point became a thriving community along the river.

When John Tenney's son Frank Folsom Tenney grew up, he operated a hotel, the Groveland House, a few hundred feet from the landing. Tourists came from the north to spend the entire winter in Federal Point. They fished in the river, ate sumptuously in the dining room, walked in the orange groves, and enjoyed the sunshine.

A large wharf was built at the landing, jutting out from the point. Farmers from Federal Point and the nearby Hastings area brought their fruit and vegetables here by wagon, drove onto the wharf, and unloaded their wares onto the steamships that traveled the St. Johns River carrying passengers, mail, and freight.

Because Palatka (originally spelled "Pilatka") was the southernmost point on the St. Johns River where oceangoing ships could safely travel, the town became an important transportation and trading hub and the main jumping-off point for travel into Florida's interior by wagon or smaller boats. Popular with visitors were excursions up the Ocklawaha River to what was one of Florida's original tourist attractions, Silver Springs.

The period between 1865 and 1895 was the golden age of Palatka—a time when the town rivaled Jacksonville as the major port on the St. Johns River. Following the Civil War, tourists who visited found new hotels, including the Putnam House, built by Hubbard L. Hart, and the Larkin House, which had accommodations for 250 guests.

In 1875, the US Post Office officially changed the spelling of "Pilatka" to "Palatka" to avoid confusion with the nearby community of Picolata. By then, several good hotels were providing fine accommodations and serving fresh food to their guests. The Arlington Hotel was one of the most popular.

This bird's-eye view of Palatka was taken in the 1880s from the top of St. Mark's Episcopal Church on Second Street. This picture was taken at a time when Palatka was at its peak as a major Florida tourist destination. Note the St. Johns River and the Putnam House hotel in the background.

The January 1876 edition of *Harper's* featured a richly written 16-page story on travels up the St. Johns River to Palatka and then further south and west up the Ocklawaha River to Silver Springs. Articles like this painted a lushly romantic picture of tropical Florida and did much to stimulate tourist traffic and motivate people to migrate to the region.

HARPER'S
NEW MONTHLY MAGAZINE.
No. CCCVIII.—JANUARY, 1876.—Vol. LII.
THE OKLAWAHA.
PALMS ON THE ST. JOHNS.

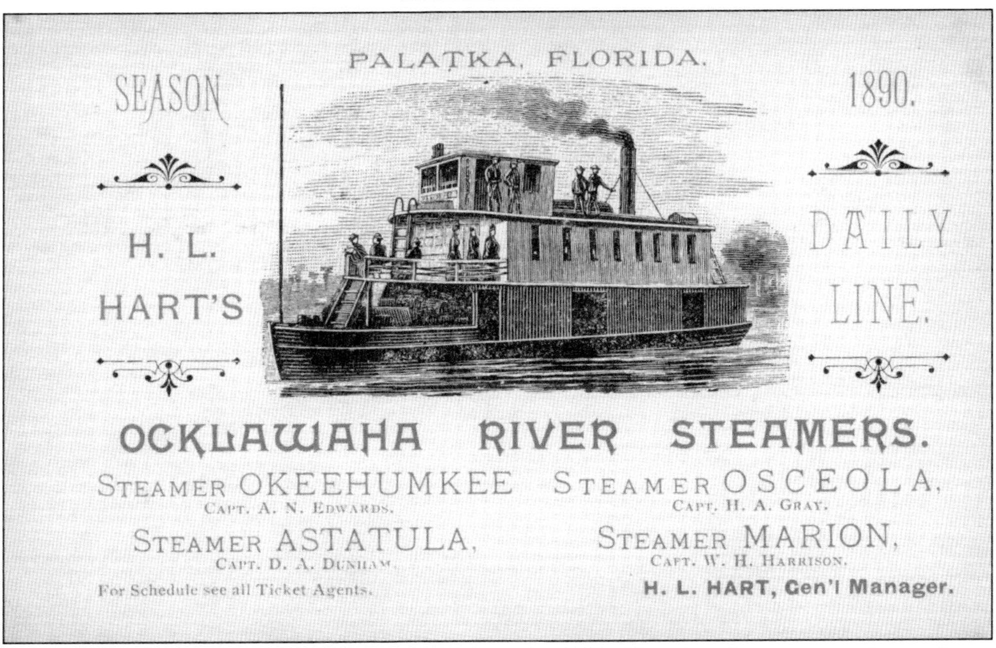

Hubbard L. Hart came to Florida from Vermont in the 1850s. Hart bought into several steamboats prior to the Civil War and, during the conflict, became a blockade runner for the Confederacy, transporting freight on the Ocklawaha and St. Johns Rivers. After the war, Hart's steamboats dominated trade and travel on the Ocklawaha. In 1880, Hart's *Osceola* transported former president Gen. Ulysses S. Grant to Silver Springs.

Ed Lucas, a Palatka entrepreneur, built the *Metamora* to compete with the Hart Line. Here, the *Metamora* is shown entering the Ocklawaha River from the St. Johns. It was a 25-mile trip from Palatka to the mouth of the Ocklawaha River and then an overnight trip to reach the junction with Silver River. From there, it was nine miles of crystal-clear waters to get to the final destination at Silver Springs.

The community of Silver Springs was founded in 1852. Soon after, the beautiful natural environment at Silver Springs began to attract visitors from throughout the United States. The springs were most commonly visited by steamer, but tourists also arrived by stagecoach and eventually by railroad. Glass-bottom boat tours of the springs began in the late 1870s.

Two

Henry Flagler, Visionary Developer of Florida

The Town of Hastings owes its existence to Standard Oil Company cofounder Henry Flagler. Flagler, along with his partner John D. Rockefeller, built Standard Oil Company into one of the world's most prominent businesses. Flagler first came to Florida for the health of his wife, Mary. In the winter of 1876, Mary's doctors suggested that Henry take her to Florida, where the climate might hasten her recovery. (Florida Memory.)

Dragging himself away from the business of Standard Oil, Henry Flagler brought his family to Florida. The Flaglers traveled by steamboat and first came to Jacksonville, where they found a wonderful climate but primitive accommodations, and there was nothing to do except walk around the dirt streets of downtown. There was not even a beach to enjoy, because the ocean was many miles away.

This photograph, looking east down Bay Street, was taken in the 1880s from the roof of the National Hotel. Several freight schooners are visible at the docks along the St. Johns River. In this era, yellow pine and cypress lumber and timber were the primary exports from the region.

Hoping to find better accommodations, Henry Flagler decided to take his family to St. Augustine, promoted as the oldest city in the United States. The family landed at the rustic Tocoi Landing, which, in 1876, must have looked very much like this photograph that was taken a few years later. (Florida Memory.)

A horsecar took the Flaglers from the landing into St. Augustine. According to an interview Henry Flagler gave to the *Jacksonville News-Herald*, the town did not make a good first impression: "We arrived at nightfall. The accommodation was very bad and most of the visitors were consumptives." In place of wholesome food, the Flaglers were served canned meat and canned vegetables. Henry disliked it so much that the family returned to Jacksonville.

This photograph of St. Augustine was taken in the 1870s or early 1880s from atop the walls of Fort Marion and looks south along the bayfront. Most of the hotels and rooming houses in this pre-Flagler era were along the bayfront or on historic St. George Street.

This photograph was also taken in the 1870s or early 1880s and looks north along the bayfront from an area near the town plaza and the building commonly known as the Slave Market. Both of these pictures give the viewer an idea of how quaint and rustic St. Augustine was before the Flagler era.

These early postcards of Charlotte and St. George Streets capture the classic Spanish Colonial look of the town. Then and now, these images typify Old St. Augustine, which was a remote outpost for Spain from the beginnings of its empire-building in the 16th century until Florida was transferred from Spain to the United States in 1821.

At left is a portrait of Henry Flagler from the 1880s. Flagler's success at the Standard Oil Company and the tremendous wealth that followed had, by this time, started to make him restless for a new challenge. As a spry 52-year-old, instead of thinking of retirement, Flagler was ready for the next great chapter in his life.

In the winter of 1882, Flagler was hospitalized with a liver condition. While recovering at his estate, he read about a land deal put together in Florida by Philadelphia industrialist Hamilton Disston. In the Federal Swamp Land Act of 1850, Florida had been given title to 13 million acres of undrained federal land. To raise money, the state made a deal with Disston, selling him four million acres for 25¢ per acre. Disston started by draining two million of the acres. Once engineers completed the first section of the drainage canal, money began to pour in for investments in major farming and livestock projects. Rail construction was also heavily promoted. During 1881 and 1882, more miles of railroad track were laid in Florida than in the previous history of the state.

Flagler decided that it was time to return to the state that was literally giving land away in exchange for development. When Flagler returned to St. Augustine in December 1883, he discovered that the town had greatly improved. According to an interview published in the *Jacksonville News-Herald* in 1887, Flagler told a friend, "I was surprised when I got there. There had been a wonderful change in the former state of things. Instead of the depressing accommodations of the years before, I found the San Marco Hotel one of the most comfortable and best-kept hotels in the world, and filled not with consumptives but with that class of society one meets at the great watering places of Europe, men who go there to enjoy themselves and not for the benefit of their health. I liked it well enough to stay and since I couldn't sit still all the time, I used to daily take walks down St. George Street, around the plaza, to the clubhouse and back to the hotel again. I found that all the other gentlemen did the same thing with the same apparent regularity because that was all there was to do for recreation and amusement. But I liked the place and I liked the climate. It occurred to me very strongly that someone with sufficient means ought to provide accommodations for the class of people who are not sick but who come here to enjoy the climate, have plenty of money but could find no satisfactory way of spending it."

By February 1885, Flagler was exploring the possibility of building a hotel designed to complement the architecture of the ancient city. In March of that year, the city of St. Augustine hosted a special costume production for visitors to celebrate the landing of Ponce de Leon in 1513. Highly impressed by the event, Flagler decided he would build a grand hotel in the center of the city and name it the Ponce de Leon. By the time Henry returned to New York in early April, he had purchased the acreage necessary for his new hotel. (Florida Memory.)

The firm of Carrere and Hastings designed the Ponce De Leon Hotel. Both John Carrere and Thomas Hastings had received their training at the Ecole Nationale Superieure des Beaux-Arts in France and had worked at the same architectural firm in New York City. The firm's first major success was the Ponce De Leon Hotel. Carrere and Hastings went on to become recognized as one of the country's outstanding Beaux-Arts architectural firms. The Ponce de Leon Hotel was finished in May 1887, but the opening was delayed until the beginning of the new winter season. With plenty of advance promotion, the hotel opened its doors on January 10, 1888, and within an hour, almost 1,000 guests were crowding the gardens and corridors of the hotel. The nation's press was in awe, as this was a hotel superior to any other in the United States. (Above, Florida Memory.)

Three

Thomas Horace Hastings

Henry Flagler began his railroad-building because he found the primitive railroads of the time insufficient for the needs of his hotels, and the state was giving away land for every mile of railroad developed. While many settlements along the railroad grew out of the efforts of small groups to establish communities, in the case of what became Hastings, Flagler himself chose to establish a model farm. In 1889, Flagler invited a distant cousin, Thomas Horace Hastings, to come to the area to raise early-harvest vegetables for the Flagler hotels.

The original tract of land developed by Thomas Horace Hastings consisted of 1,569 acres on which he built a two-and-a-half-story house for his family. He named the farm Prairie Garden—a name derived, in part, from a reference to Rose Prairie, a nearby area that had recently been platted by Park Terrell, an Iowa farmer who had also seen the potential in the rich bottomlands.

Thomas Hastings also built a glass greenhouse to grow cucumbers and other vegetables. In a 1940 letter, Hastings's daughter Elsie wrote, "My father cleared a large tract of land upon which he built a house and log cabins for the families of the foremen and workers, large greenhouses and a log cabin playhouse for me. My father shipped strawberries and vegetables, especially cucumbers, to New York hotels during the winter season."

In October 1891, the postal service opened an office at Hastings. That year, reports of Thomas Hastings's achievements appeared in Florida's official horticultural journal, and in 1892, they showed up in a US Congressional document. These reports brought much attention to southwest St. Johns County as a viable farming community. The availability of artesian wells, rich soils, and a temperate climate encouraged settlement, and the expansion of farming began in the area.

Agriculture soon became the area's dominant industry, and potatoes became the crop of choice for many of the county's farmers, especially after devastating freezes swept into Florida during the mid-1890s and severely damaged citrus crops. Other important industries of the time included cattle and turpentine production.

George Waterman Leonard was born in Bridgewater, Massachusetts. Reared in the farming tradition, Leonard relocated in 1883 to Lowell, Florida, a settlement in Marion County. While there, Leonard developed some of the first holdings of the Wetumpka Fruit Company of Boston and served as its manager. George Waterman Leonard and his wife, Emma Jeanette (Billings) Leonard, with baby Faith, are shown in the center of this stereoview photograph taken in Lowell.

The Leonards moved to Hastings in October 1895, a year that coincided with the devastating freezes in December 1894 and February 1895. Pictured here around 1900 in front of their Hastings home are (first row, seated) Aunt Perkins, Lucy, and George; (second row, standing) Flossie, Stella, Lewis, George V., and Emma.

Wetumpka Fruit Co.,

HASTINGS, FLA.

THE LARGEST FARM IN ST. JOHNS CO.

200 Acres under cultivation.
30 Acres in Bearing Grove.
20 Acres will bear in two years.
100 Head cattle.

RESIDENCE OF GEORGE W. LEONARD, MANAGER OF THE WETUMPKA FRUIT CO.'S FARM, HASTINGS, FLA.

Adjoining the cultivated land we have several hundred acres of the same quality of land as that in cultivation, which we will dispose of at a low price, to actual settlers. These lands all have outside ditches and are first-class in every particular. Last year we shipped 4,500 barrels cabbage, 1,503 barrels Irish potatoes, 100 barrels squash, 3,000 bushels sweet potatoes, 100 boxes oranges, 24 barrels syrup, saving seed for 15 acres. We raised 600 bushels oats, 800 bushels corn, 40 tons hay. *We have no cultivated lands for sale.* To first-class families we will make special prices on any size tract. Two and one-half miles from depot; good school and church in immediate vicinity. One of the best neighborhoods in the State. Address

GEORGE W. LEONARD,
Hastings, Florida.

Henry Flagler promoted Hastings as a farming community not only so fresh vegetables could be produced for guests staying at his fashionable hotels but also to provide income for his railroad to transport crops to market. Through the *Florida East Coast Homeseeker*, a newspaper issued by Flagler's land companies, Flagler disseminated information about Florida's agriculture, coastal communities, and mild weather. This advertisement ran in the *Florida East Coast Homeseeker* edition of 1899.

Because of Henry Flagler's influence, people began to speculate on land throughout northeastern Florida, and Flagler's Model Land Company was overwhelmed with offers. This is the cover of a popular real estate brochure produced by the Gem City Improvement Company of Dayton, Ohio, promoting the sale of land in the Hastings area. (Mary Murphy.)

OF ALL the old Southern States, no other State is attracting so many homeseekers, and so much money for investment as the State of Florida today. Men from every section of the United States are casting their eyes toward the "Sunny South." The Southbound trains these days are crowded with people from the North and West, going to the South to buy land and make investments.

This is the opening paragraph of the Gem City Improvement Company's sales brochure entitled "Farm and Truck Lands in the Famous Hastings Potato District." Gem City Improvement Company promoted Hastings as "a progressive town of about 1,200 people on the Florida East Coast Railway, 54 miles south of Jacksonville—the New York of the South." (Mary Murphy.)

This is an early photograph of Hastings looking south down Main Street (the boy in the foreground is Charnalle Campbell). The Hastings train depot was to the right and out of view. The newly built Hastings Hotel is on the left. The first bank in Hastings was located on the ground floor of the hotel building. The E.G. Coe Pharmacy is on the left about halfway down the block.

This is a look inside the E.G. Coe Pharmacy, with Coe shown leaning on the counter for the benefit of the photographer. A closer inspection shows patent remedies, herbs, and other natural medicines and even a selection of Cuban cigars. Pres. Warren G. Harding was a classmate of Coe's. Harding visited the Coes in Hastings when he came to Florida. (Nancy Towns.)

This early photograph shows one of the Hastings railway station docks with a farmer supervising the transfer of barrels of potatoes, which had been brought to town by horse and wagon, to boxcars bound for markets across the nation. (Michelle West Hicks.)

This c. 1908 photograph shows a long line of boxcars being loaded with barrels of Hastings potatoes—something that would become a common sight for decades to come. The railroad station and the newly built Hastings Hotel are visible in the distance.

This is a photograph of the Florida East Coast Railway stationmaster for the Hastings depot in front of his home shortly after 1900. Becoming a stop on the Florida East Coast Railway provided the spark that caused many farming communities to develop along the east coast of Florida. (Nancy Towns.)

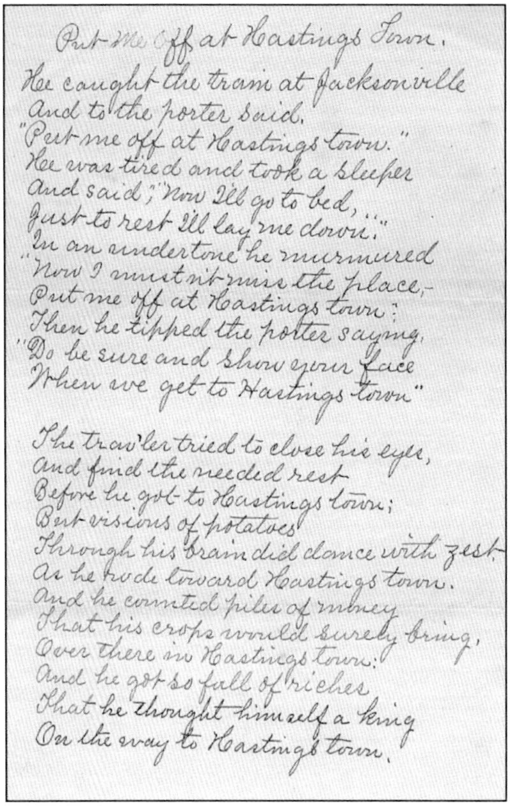

Put Me Off at Hastings Town.

Hee caught the train at Jacksonville
And to the porter said,
"Put me off at Hastings town."
Hee was tired and took a sleeper
And said, "Now I'll go to bed,
Just to rest I'll lay me down."
In an undertone he murmured
"Now I must n't miss the place,-
Put me off at Hastings town:"
Then he tipped the porter saying,
"Do be sure and show your face
When we get to Hastings town"

The trav'ler tried to close his eyes,
And find the needed rest
Before he got to Hastings town;
But visions of potatoes
Through his brain did dance with zest,
As he rode toward Hastings town.
And he counted piles of money
That his crops would surely bring,
Over there in Hastings town:
And he got so full of riches
That he thought himself a king
On the way to Hastings town.

These photographs show a poem written by M.A. Taylor in 1900 praising the riches soon to be found at Hastings. The poem describes a weary traveler taking the train from Jacksonville to Hastings who is afraid that he will fall asleep and miss his stop. The second stanza says, "The trav'ler tried to close his eyes, / And find the needed rest / Before he got to Hastings town: / But visions of potatoes / Through his brain did dance with zest, / As he rode toward Hastings town. / And he counted piles of money / That his crops would surely bring, / Over there in Hastings town. / And he got so full of riches / That he thought himself a king / On the way to Hastings town."

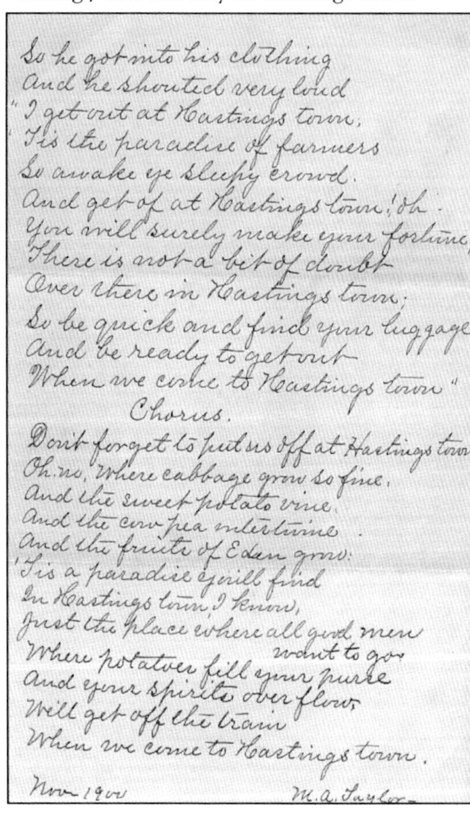

So he got into his clothing
And he shouted very loud
"I get out at Hastings town;
'Tis the paradise of farmers
So awake ye sleepy crowd.
And get of at Hastings town! Oh.
You will surely make your fortune,
There is not a bit of doubt
Over there in Hastings town;
So be quick and find your luggage
And be ready to get out
When we come to Hastings town"

Chorus.

Don't forget to put us off at Hastings town
Oh no, where cabbage grow so fine.
And the sweet potato vine.
And the cow pea intertwine.
And the fruits of Edan grow:
'Tis a paradise ye will find
In Hastings town, I know,
Just the place where all good men want to go
Where potatoes fill your purse
And your spirits overflow,
Will get off the train
When we come to Hastings town.

Nov 1900 M.A. Taylor

The first Methodist Church services in Hastings began around 1898 in what was known as the Town Hall, a building about a mile from Hastings on the Daytona Road. The St. Johns Methodist Episcopal Church building, shown here in 1904, was located about a half mile south of town. The message on this postcard reads: "This is the place where Hastings Potatoes are raised, did you ever here [*sic*] of them?"

This postcard from 1909 shows a group of potato buyers gathered in front of a boardinghouse—appropriately named the Travelers Home—in Hastings. The note on the postcard says: "I am in this group, see if you can find me & Ella."

This mule-drawn wagon is holding 36 barrels of Irish potatoes (the record for a single wagonload of potatoes was 40 barrels). Grower T.B. "Ted" Glass is standing in front of the wagon, J.G.B. Smith is in the back of the wagon, and the man sitting atop the barrels is unidentified. (Nancy Towns.)

By 1900, Hastings was a thriving boomtown. During the harvest season, potatoes packed in barrels were loaded at a rate of over 60 boxcars a day. Some historians who have chronicled the area have said that in its heyday, Hastings would occasionally ship more than 100 boxcars of potatoes in a single day.

The Hastings Hotel opened in 1908. Guests could pass the time on the second-floor porch talking with other guests or listening to a band playing in the gazebo a short distance away. Businessmen in suits discussed the potato crop over lunch in the dining room, contrasting with farmers in their work clothes who were in town to buy a needed piece of equipment or tool from Farmer's Supply.

In 1910, the east side of Main Street had the Hughes building, which housed E.G. Coe's Pharmacy, the Hughes department store, the Oliver Plow Company, a millinery store, and the post office.

On the west side of Main Street were the telephone office, the Hastings Cold Storage building, and Alex Middleton's mercantile store, which is shown here. (Michelle West Hicks.)

For many years, Hastings potatoes were dug by hand, as shown in this picture taken at Springwood Farms, which was located near Hastings. It was not until 1945 that the first mechanical harvester was tested in Florida by two Hastings growers who used a homemade one-row machine that placed potatoes in bags. (St. Augustine Historical Society Research Library.)

Until recently, potato seed was cut by hand from larger potatoes unless small B-sized potatoes were available. Here, baby Richard Beck is in the arms of his maternal grandmother, Fannie Drennon Mead (at left) while she and an unidentified woman cut seed potatoes for planting. (Mary Jo Beck Perry.)

This is a scene from Edgefield-on-the-St.-Johns at Orange Mills, with Cecil Murphy driving the tractor and Henry Kitt riding the potato digger. Henry Kitt and his wife, Mattie, also operated a small general store in Orange Mills. Henry was tragically killed when he was struck by a hit-and-run driver while helping a stranded motorist. (Mary Murphy.)

Edgefield-on-the-St.-Johns matriarch Maggie Josephine Hazel Murphy (right) and Thomas ? stand in one of the Edgefield potato fields about 1920. The best year for Edgefield-on-the-St.-Johns was 1925. When the Great Depression happened a few years later, the Murphy family lost most of their former wealth. (Mary Murphy.)

Although the automobile was invented during the 1890s, the new horseless carriage only began to be commercialized after the turn of the century. At that time, roads throughout the country were primitive, and horse-drawn buggies were the most popular means of transportation. This photograph of the Palatka Road, looking west from Hastings, is typical of the roadways of the time—but big changes were about to happen.

Four

THE DIXIE HIGHWAY ERA

In 1916, the first paved roadway in the Southeast was completed through St. Johns County. Called the Dixie Highway, the roadway came south from Jacksonville through St. Augustine, turned southwest and followed a route into Hastings, then turned southeast going to Ormond Beach and then down the coast to Miami. With the Dixie Highway running down Main Street in Hastings, it literally put the small community on the map.

In 1916, a parade celebrating the opening of the Dixie Highway created great excitement throughout the region. A parade of 40 automobiles adorned with bunting and flags departed from St. Augustine and was led by I.I. Moody, A.H. Faver, and W.B. Edminster into Hastings and later continued along the brick-paved Dixie Highway into Daytona. Moody had strongly encouraged construction of the highway while serving as chairman of the St. Johns County Commission in 1913 and 1914.

Citizens at Elkton and Hastings paid tribute to the motorcade as it passed through their communities. Prizes were awarded for the best-decorated vehicles, and locals from the surrounding community joined in and decorated their horses, buggies, and wagons.

During the 1916 parade, a crowd congregated in front of the Hastings Cold Storage building (above), where a band played and local politicians made speeches praising progress and what the roadway would mean for the town, the county, and the state. Highway officials complimented the St. Johns County commissioners on their wonderful achievement in road-building. After the parade, the community capped off the event with a town barbecue and a baseball game between two popular area teams at the local baseball park (below). This was the era in which baseball was truly the national pastime, and every community had its own hometown team.

The Florida Fertile Lands Company, managed by James Parkhill, was another major promoter of farmland sales in Hastings and the surrounding area. Each photograph in Parkhill's brochure, produced in 1917, shows the tall Parkhill in one of the fields or in front of an attractive local home. (Wayne Smith.)

This photograph shows James Parkhill standing in a field of potatoes ready to be harvested at one of the community's many successful farms. Parkhill resided in St. Augustine but maintained land offices in both St. Augustine and Hastings. His promotion of area farmlands through photographs like this inspired farming families from other parts of the country to move to the area. (Wayne Smith.)

The O.C. Dinkins family arrived in Hastings in 1912, but O.C. died in 1913, leaving his widow to her own resources. In 1915, she contracted with a firm that agreed to supply her with seed and fertilizer provided that the company sold her crop. After the harvest and deducting commissions and the cost of seed, fertilizer, labor, and barrels, Mrs. Dinkins cleared a sizeable profit of $7,633. (Wayne Smith.)

The Parkhill family is shown standing next to the recently completed Dixie Highway. The Dixie Highway was a one-lane road paved with oversized bricks made from Alabama red clay. Automobiles had to pull off to the side in order to pass one another. A nine-mile section of the original road still exists today as one of the back roads to Bunnell a few miles outside of Hastings off County Road 13.

Oranges, grapefruit, and other citrus had a place of importance at several farms in the county. This photograph shows, from left to right, Fred M. Leonard with George V. Leonard (son of George Waterman Leonard) and Florence and Myron Howard standing in one of the Wetumpka Fruit Company orange groves in Hastings in 1918.

In addition to planting potatoes and oranges, farmers planted various truck crops, including cabbage, celery, cucumbers, corn, peas, and tomatoes. In 1923, in a move indicative of the agricultural growth of St. Johns County, the University of Florida established the Hastings Potato Investigations Laboratory, which was initially housed in rented buildings. In 1927, the Hastings Potato Growers Association donated land on which the University of Florida developed a laboratory building, greenhouse, and storage buildings.

Celery was another crop investigated by some local farmers. Here, Joe Flake is shown in his Model A Ford truck driving his celery crop to be loaded on a boxcar for shipment. While celery was never a leading crop in Hastings, it did become a major crop about 100 miles farther south in the town of Sanford on the shores of Lake Monroe. Sanford is still nicknamed the "Celery City."

Cucumbers became one of the first crops cultivated by Thomas Horace Hastings in 1890. Other growers also experimented with cucumbers, including George Waller, a potato broker and supplier of farm implements who is easily identifiable in photographs thanks to his trademark Panama hat. Originally a produce merchant in Philadelphia, Waller left the wholesale business in the northeast for the farmlands of St. Johns County in 1909.

Tomatoes were also cultivated on some local farms. Although tomatoes were not grown as a commercial crop in the United States until the 1870s, tomato production in the country started on the southwest coast of Florida in Manatee County and slowly spread to other farming areas in the state.

James Parkhill (center) is shown here with unidentified business associates in one of the area's cornfields. Corn was a popular second crop for some potato growers and also served as a cover crop to help add nutrients to the soil between plantings. (Wayne Smith.)

Cattle ranching has been an important industry in the region since 1655, when the Spanish colonial government began developing the area that would become Palatka, Gainesville, and Tallahassee into three principal ranching areas to feed Spanish settlers, particularly those in St. Augustine, where the slaughterhouses were located.

Between 1911 and 1915, the state's leading newspaper, *Jacksonville's Florida Times-Union*, increasingly covered the potato crop in Hastings. The "Hastings Potato" reigned supreme, and the total yield of the annual harvest continued to make the point that the Hastings area had truly become "Florida's Potato Capital."

This farmer is harvesting his potato crop and taking the potatoes straight from the field through a Boggs Grader (an invention used by many Hastings growers) and into the potato barrels in which they would soon be shipped by steamer or rail. (Nancy Towns.)

For many years, barrels were the preferred container in which to ship potatoes. The Whitehouse Barrel Company and the Nix Produce Company (pictured here) located their barrel-manufacturing facilities at the end of Railroad Avenue near the Florida East Coast Railway depot in Hastings.

Potato buyers and sellers are shown tracking the location of Nix Produce Company's boxcars as they travel to their destinations. Every pin denotes the location of a boxcar of Hastings potatoes in transit to markets across the country.

In 1918, a scarcity of potatoes boosted the price to $20 a barrel. Growers harvested an unusually large crop, and buyers and commission men from all parts of the country rushed in and paid cash for their purchases. The bank deposits were so heavy that town officials patrolled the streets each night and remained on duty until armored trucks arrived in the morning to transfer the cash to Jacksonville banks.

The 1918 influenza pandemic (which lasted from around January 1918 to December 1920), also known as the Spanish flu, was an unusually deadly virus that infected 500 million people around the world. In Hastings, the Red Cross organized a group of local volunteers who were trained in how to best care for their families and other members of the community.

Women's suffrage was an international movement with the goal of ensuring the right of women to vote. The contribution of women during World War I made it difficult to maintain the idea that women were—by constitution and temperament—unfit to vote. Supporters of the movement are shown here in the Hastings area rallying before the ratification of the 19th Amendment in 1920. (Nancy Towns.)

Stonestreet and Miller was one of the first automobile repair shops in Hastings. True to the time of the transition from horse and buggy to automobile, Stonestreet and Miller also provided blacksmith and metalworking services. (Nancy Towns.)

The first automobile dealership in town was the Hastings Motor Company, originally owned by Manson Waller. Christopher Stanton Sr. and Charles Garrett bought the company in 1924, and it continued under that name until the bank failed and the business went under at the beginning of the Depression in 1929. (Nancy Towns.)

The Ford dealership reopened in November 1929 under the name of Stanton Motors and continued as a prominent business in the community for over 50 years. Christopher Stanton's son Charles returned to Hastings in 1955 after serving in the armed forces and joined his father in the business. Charles eventually became president of the company, and the business greatly contributed to the economy of Hastings. (Chris Stanton.)

Like the automobile dealerships in large cities, the interior of Stanton Motors included a showroom where one could shop for new cars; a waiting area for customers; and the parts department, featured here. (Chris Stanton.)

Five

The Hub of a Major Farming Community

From a 21st-century perspective, it can be difficult to appreciate just how "thriving" the Hastings community was prior to the Great Depression. Most of southwestern St. Johns County was farmland, and Hastings was the commercial hub for a prosperous area that included the farming communities of Elkton, Armstrong, Spuds, Orange Mills, and Federal Point. (Nancy Towns.)

In 1925, the Florida East Coast Railway double-tracked its mainline between Jacksonville and Miami. Increased traffic along Florida's east coast necessitated the expansion, which included a new, more eastern route south, effectively bypassing Elkton, Hastings, and Palatka. Still, the company continued to maintain and invest in the old route. This is a photograph of the Hastings railway depot in 1929. (Nancy Towns.)

Trains, like the Potato Special pictured here, passed through Hastings around 20 to 30 times a day carrying freight and passengers. During the Florida land boom of the 1920s, the Florida East Coast Railway gave colorful names to its locomotives. Their most popular passenger trains were the Dixie Flyer, the Key West Express, and the Everglades Limited.

During the digging season, an army of potato buyers would flock from across the country to Hastings to bid for the community's produce. This photograph shows a number of potato buyers, including Ansley Hall Sr. (second from left).

Main Street in Hastings was lined with stores selling hardware, drugs, groceries, and clothing. Other businesses included the Big Brick Garage, Hastings Cold Storage Company, and Langford's Garage. The town even had its own newspaper, the *Hastings Herald*.

The Hastings Herald Publishing Company produced the weekly *Hastings Herald* newspaper. James Augustus Wallace Sr., editor of the *Hastings Herald*, is pictured around 1915. (Shirley Stone.)

D. Willard McElveen is shown with his Farmer's Supply delivery truck. Prior to the 1920s, McElveen owned the Farmer's Supply hardware store in the Hughes Building. He later sold that business and opened McElveen Hardware, which was a popular shopping destination for farmers, homeowners, and sportsmen for many years due to its selection of hunting and fishing supplies. (Nancy Towns.)

Many businesses were important to the community of Hastings, including Lovett's Market. Bob Lovett's grocery store was a fixture on Main Street from 1926 until Lovett retired in 1982. Lovett later became active in local politics, serving on the city council and as mayor of Hastings, and he eventually represented southwestern St. Johns County as a county commissioner.

Elmo Causey came to Hastings right after leaving high school in Newnan, Georgia, to work in the drugstore then owned by Lance Freeman. Causey bought the drugstore after Dr. Freeman died, and it became known as Elmo's. Elmo's was a center of activity in Hastings. Farmers would finish their early morning chores and then, every day around 10:00 a.m., go to Elmo's for coffee and conversation.

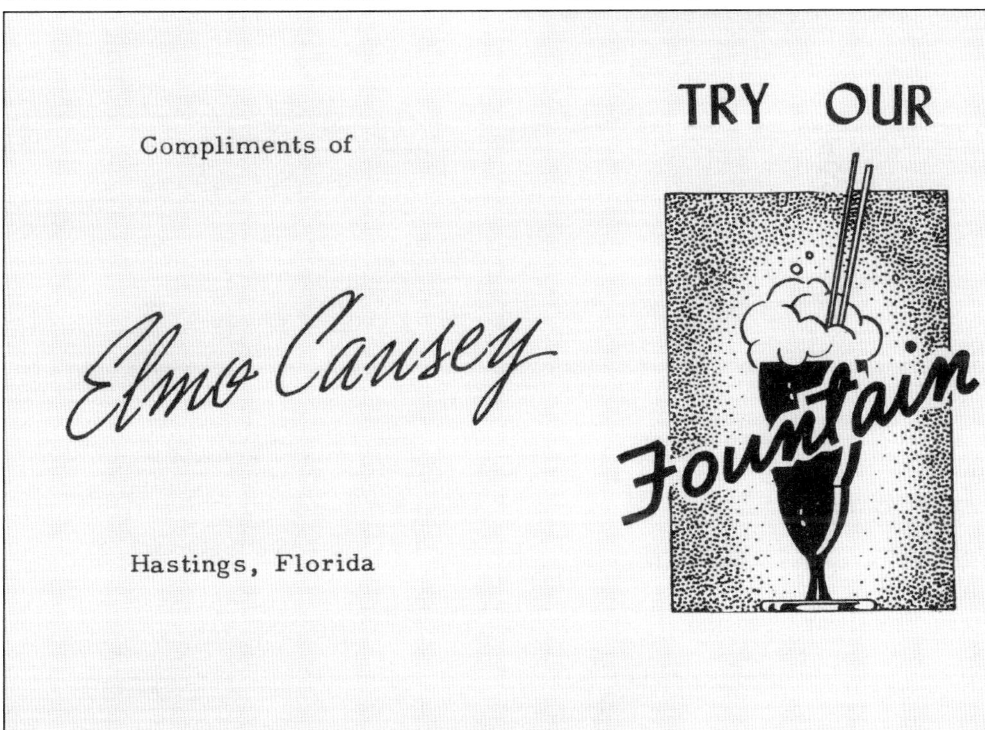

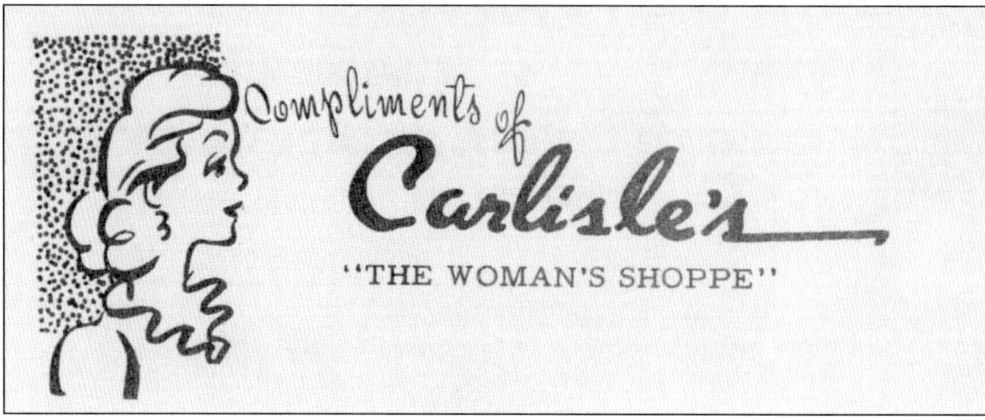

Another institution in Hastings was Carlisle's Dress Shop. Rhoda Johnson Carlisle opened her exclusive dress shop in the 1920s in the old bank building on Main Street. Ladies from Palatka, St. Augustine, Jacksonville, and other surrounding communities came to Hastings to enjoy Miss Rhoda's lovely shop.

Rhoda Carlisle was well ahead of her time, providing many women with the services of a personal shopper. Her business was a notable success in Hastings for almost 50 years and was only sold after Carlisle's health failed.

The "Famous Hastings Potato District" also attracted some of the tourists traveling down the east coast of Florida. Here, members of the Elmer Whitney family from Toledo, Ohio, enjoyed having their picture taken in a Hastings orange grove in 1930. (Florida Memory.)

Improved highways and automobiles brought increased numbers of tourists to Florida during the Great Depression. This photograph shows Elmer Smith and his son Donald picking grapefruit in a Hastings grove in 1930. (Florida Memory.)

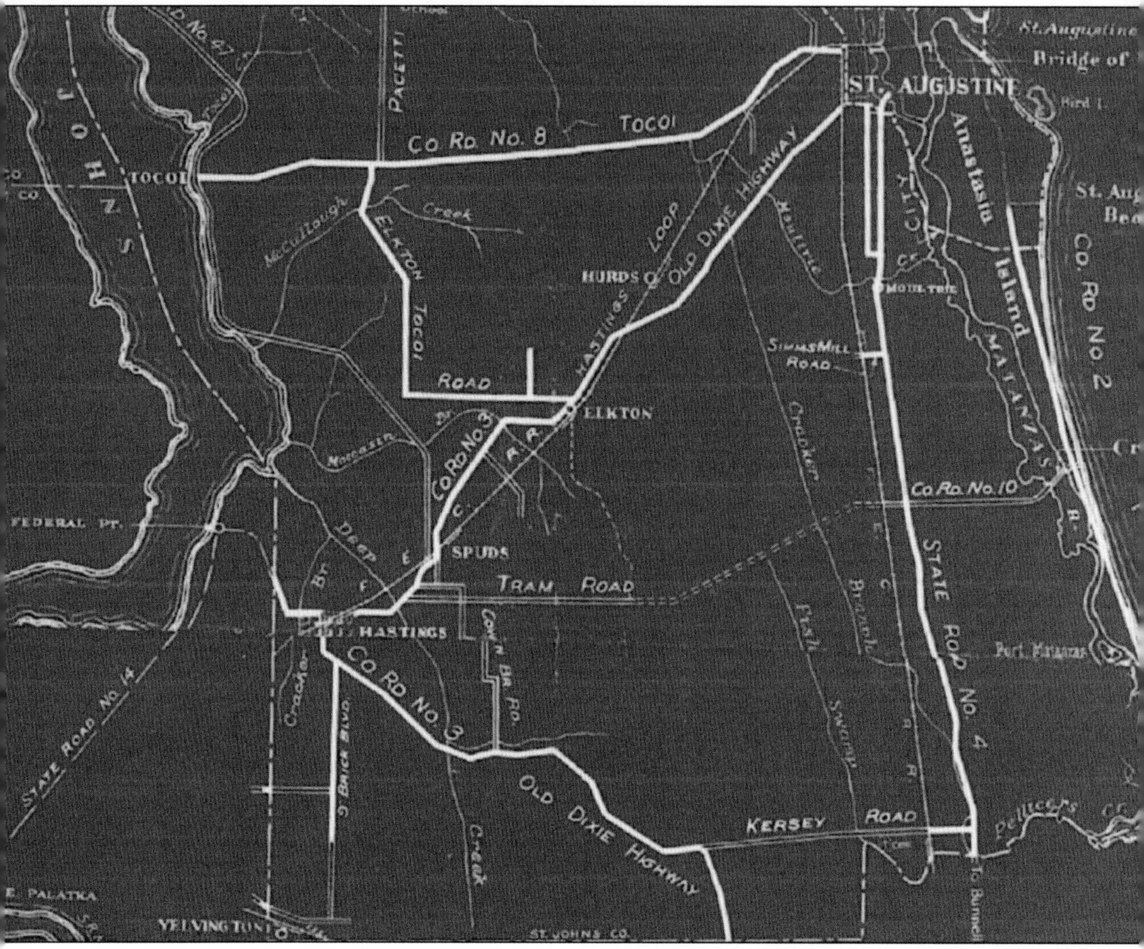

The Dixie Highway, which ran through Hastings, served as the primary route of travel for tourists motoring along Florida's east coast until 1925, when a new alignment for the Dixie Highway shortened the route and brought travelers due south from St. Augustine. This map shows the original circuitous route through Elkton and Hastings as well as the new Dixie Highway, shown here as "State Road No. 4," which would later become US Route 1.

In 1927, the newly organized Hastings Potato Growers Cooperative developed a distinctive building north of the downtown area. Operating as the Hastings Potato Growers Association, the cooperative advanced funds to farmers to grow crops and also helped with the sales and marketing of their harvests.

Harvesting Irish Potatoes at Hastings, Fla.

This postcard is from the era shortly after mechanical tractors began to replace mule-drawn farm implements for the planting and maintenance of potato crops. Mechanization greatly reduced the labor required to grow and harvest potatoes, which, until the 1950s, were harvested by hand.

This aerial photograph provides an overview of the Wetumpka Fruit Company farm. The home of farm manager George V. Leonard and his wife, Lillie, is on the far left. Moving clockwise, the next building was the home of George's brother Lewis; his wife, Elizabeth; and their daughter Phyllis, who later became Wetumpka's secretary and treasurer. In the top center of the photograph is the home of Bill and Mary Ethel Cotton. In the lower right corner is the Wetumpka potato packinghouse, and in the center at the bottom is the home of Vernon and Juanita Tines.

Citrus crate labels from Wetumpka Fruit Company exhibited artwork reminiscent of beautiful grove-and-river scenes at Hastings. The company marketed its products under the "Prairie Flower" label and the "Prairie Garden" label, a name derived from Hastings' earliest history. The company shipped citrus to northern markets by boat from its citrus packinghouse in Hastings. By the early 1930s, the company maintained a grove of 338 acres, which was one of the largest citrus holdings in St. Johns County.

The Wetumpka Fruit Company citrus packinghouse was at the south end of the Hastings farm, and during the winter, picking and packing season was always bustling with activity. Packinghouses like this served an important community function throughout Florida, as it provided a service for the smaller growers who were unable to finance their own packing facilities.

This view from the roof of the Wetumpka Fruit Company citrus packinghouse shows the orange and grapefruit groves extending far into the distance. In the springtime, when the citrus trees in Hastings and Federal Point were in bloom, the entire community was filled with the sweet scent of orange blossoms. All of these trees were destroyed in January 1983, when temperatures dropped to single digits, eliminating all commercial citrus production north of Orlando.

Early in its development, the Leonard farm established a strong relationship with the Florida Agricultural Experiment Station and the University of Florida. According to research consultants Bland & Associates, "The Leonards' contacts with Florida's premier institution of higher learning and foremost agricultural experts helped make their farm among the most productive and successful in the state." (Florida Memory.)

The increased use of mechanical harvesters influenced the development of the equipment needed in a potato packinghouse. The average packinghouse had bins for storage prior to grading, where custom work, washing, drying, sizing, and packaging for fresh market sales were done. Here, a woman checks for defects as potatoes travel along the grading line at the Wetumpka potato packinghouse in 1947. (Florida Memory.)

In the course of the history of potato production in the Hastings area, potatoes have been packed in barrels, baskets, and burlap bags based on the economics and preferences of the buyers of the times. This photograph shows a farmworker packing a potato basket at the Wetumpka potato packinghouse. (Florida Memory.)

George W. Leonard, grandson of George Waterman Leonard, is shown posing for a photographer from the Florida Department of Agriculture with a market basket of Prairie Garden potatoes at the Wetumpka potato packinghouse. (Florida Memory.)

One of the special events each year in the farming community was the crowning of the Potato Queen. This is a promotional photograph of Peggy Davis, the Potato Queen of 1946, resting on a bed of potatoes.

Part of the Potato Queen tradition was for the queen to be photographed in a wardrobe made from burlap potato bags. Here, Peggy Davis is dressed for the part.

For young women who were not old enough to compete for the Potato Queen crown, there was the Miss Potato Blossom competition.

If potatoes were the No. 1 crop in southwest St. Johns County, then cabbage was a very important No. 2. This exhibit depicts St. Johns County farmers heralding Hastings and Elkton as "Florida's Cabbage Capital." By the middle of the 20th century, the Hastings region was shipping more than 1.4 million crates of cabbages each year.

The photographs on this page were taken for a brochure promoting cabbage production in Elkton sometime in the late 1940s. These pictures glamorize the hard work of growing, harvesting, and bringing this crop to market. The image at right shows Peggy McCormick tending the cabbage in a field. (Florida Memory.)

By 1949, St. Johns County contained 136 farms planted with 3,574 acres of cabbage. Here, Jane Gardner (right) and Peggy McCormick are shown bagging "Fresh Green" brand cabbages from Elkton. (Florida Memory.)

The Hastings Potato Growers Association also harvested and packed cabbage for area growers, using a distinctive crate label to identify its products. This photograph shows a wagonload of cabbages being bagged, weighed, and stacked in preparation for the trip to market. (Florida Memory.)

Here, two farm workers add one last bag to an outbound truck filled with fresh Elkton cabbages. (Florida Memory.)

Six

SCHOOLS

The first school in Hastings opened around 1897, but the student population grew so rapidly that it was soon necessary to construct a larger school. The Old School House, pictured here, opened in 1900. When it opened, the two-story building was composed of only four rooms. Later, an additional wing and bell tower were added. Ella Smith was the first teacher who taught in this building.

This is the third-grade class of 1920–1921 at the Old Hastings School. Pictured are, from left to right, (first row) teacher Annabelle Robinson, Betty Leonard, Margaret Beck, Ruth Campbell, and Frances McElveen; (second row) Helen Heath, Margarette Goodwin, unidentified, Netha Campbell, James Gable, and Adrin Beach; (third row) Wilbur Bailey, Bill Sellers, Lloyd Miller, Virgil Mathis, Glen Curtis, and Frank Robshaw. Many of these children were members of the Hastings graduating class of 1931. (Nancy Towns.)

Students pose in front of the Old Hastings School in 1923. The students from this class who later graduated from Hastings High School in 1933 were (in alphabetical order) Ivan Brown, Eeslie Brubaker, June Green, Beatrice Hawley, Edward Kaiser, Kenneth McKinney, Mary Kinsey, George W. Leonard, Jennings W. Minton, Merle Mimms, Warren Stevens, Ruby Smith, and Anna Vallance.

This is a photo collage documenting the opening of the new Hastings High School in 1925. A parade was organized for schoolchildren, residents, and several marching bands to travel from the Old Hastings School to the new one. Clockwise from top left are the Scottish Highlander Band, the Hastings Hotel and the old post office, children in the parade, and the military band; the new Hastings High School is in the center. (Charlotte Wilke Markham.)

Hastings High School contained all 12 grades and also educated students about the commercial and agricultural subjects needed for those not planning to attend college. The south wing housed grades one through six, and the north wing contained grades seven through twelve. In 1926, the first graduating class of the new school included Virginia Gable, Ellen Hart Johnson, George Martin, Mary Catherine Middleton, Agnes Minton, and Miriam Smith Wyllys.

This is a January 1935 photograph of teacher Lula Mae Campbell's third-grade class. (Nancy Towns.)

Teacher Virginia Campbell's third-grade class is shown here in 1938. Pictured are, from left to right, (first row) Harry Wilharm, Charles Barnum, Jonelle Tanner, Richard Maltby, Clyde Kersey, John Beck, Mary Eddins, and unidentified; (second row) Charles Burrell, Annabelle Kersey, Bobby Hough, Mary Alice Wolfe, James Smyly, Wilma Leverett, Helen Hough, Thelma Johnson, and Maratha ?; (third row) Junior Tomlinson, David Strunk, Glen Bradbury, Minnie Dixon, Glen Wallace, Mae Rountree, Eloed Moody, Barbara Morris, Millard Browning, Charles Stanton, and Ray Odom.

The first graduating class of the Old Hastings School is pictured here in 1906 (the Old Hastings School only went up to the 10th grade). Margaret Avent was the teacher. The graduates are, from left to right, Ethel DuPont, Eva McCullough, Hazel DuPont, Florence Leonard, George V. Leonard, Verna McCullough, Marion Seymour, Eula McCullough, and Stella Leonard; not pictured are Courtland Flake, Hazel Flake, and Braden Purcell. (Tracey Jozokos.)

The Hastings High School graduating class of 1931 pictured here included, from left to right, Ruth Campbell, Pauline Kirkpatrick, Martha Middleton, Dorothy Yelvington, Emma Lowe, Virgil Mathis, Bill Sellers, Christine McClinton (sponsor), Dick Gray, N.D. Killingsworth, Frances McElveen, Netha Campbell, Margaret Beck, and Vermel King. (Nancy Towns.)

The Hastings High School graduating class of 1934 shown here included, from left to right, (first row) Helen Brocklehurst, Helen Deford, Evelyn Reid, and Miriam Ivey; (second row) E.W. "Dub" Causey, Stanton Kuter, Fletcher Campbell, Arthur Pellicer, William "Gus" Thomas, Benjamin Padgett, and Charles McCullar. (Nancy Towns.)

Pictured is the Hastings High School graduating class of 1941. They are, from left to right, (first row) Wanda Keller, Thelma Griffin, Gianetta Kersey, Gladys Curtis, Faustina Triay, and Margaret Stevens; (second row) Francis Beach, Alton Roberts, James McCallum, Royce Masters, Dennis Lopez, and Bernard Badger. (Nancy Towns.)

This is the Hastings High School graduating class of 1942. They are, from left to right, (first row) Billie Brough, Anne Bundick, Harriett Yelvington, Ruth Hedrick, and Gerald Allen; (second row) Irene Kerseg, Ethel Mae Wells, Carolyn Flewellen, Bernice Goodwin, Freda Lovett, Yolanda Allen, and Frederick Kaiser; (third row) Edward Keller, Robley Miles, Warren Godwin, James Messervey, and Leon Cain. (Charlotte Wilke Markham.)

The Hastings High School Beta Club of 1946–1947 is pictured here. They are, from left to right, (first row) David McCubbin, unidentified, and Tommy Cain; (second row) Betty Wyllys, unidentified, sponsor Mae Campbell, Nellie Mae Wallace, unidentified, Vera Beach, Pat Thomas, Cassie Griffin, and Lucille Robertson; (third row) Charles Stanton, Lester Hall, two unidentified young men, Benny Maltby, and unidentified. (Chris Stanton.)

The Hastings High School concert and marching band was well-known throughout the region. Pictured here in 1957 are, from left to right, (first row) majorette Carole Johnson, drum majorette Dianne Masters, and and majorette Sally Norris. The band members behind them are (first row) Charleen McElveen, Edna Jean Wright, Jack McCullough, Roy Johnson, Mary Jo Beck, Susan Burrell, Amy Ray Beach, and Jacqueline McCullar; (second row) Bonnie Brown, John Pacetti, Gregory Magarian, Sharon McCullar, Candy Hampton, Mary Ellen Masters, Ruby Moody, Dorothy Carmean, Kay Reynolds, Cheri Maltby, Nancy Hedrick, Mary Ellen Tomlinson, Marsha Masters, Sylvia Bailey, and Sandra Cornelison; (third row) Frances Parish, Gayle Maltby, Patsy Brantley, Sammy Lane, Anne Yarborough, LaTrelle Anderson, and Randy Greene. W.H. Coleman was the band director.

The Hastings High School band marched everywhere. It marched at football games and paraded through the downtown streets of Hastings, as shown here in the fall of 1957. The drum majorette was Dianne Masters, the other majorettes were Carole Johnson and Sally Norris, and the color guard was Grant Holland and Lee Maltby. (Nancy Towns.)

The Hastings High School band marched down St. George Street during the annual Easter parade in St. Augustine. Shown here along with the band are drum majorette Diana Hartline and majorettes Dianne Masters and Sally Norris. (Nancy Towns.)

The Hastings High School majorettes in the fall of 1957 were Carole Johnson (left), drum majorette Dianne Masters (center), and Sally Norris. (Nancy Towns.)

The Hastings High School majorettes in the fall of 1961 were Pat Beck (left), drum majorette Frances Parish (center), and Patsy Turney. (Nancy Towns.)

At the Hastings High School junior Christmas dance in December 1958, Patsy Masters (right), Miss Merry Christmas of 1957, crowned Virginia Brown as Miss Merry Christmas of 1958.

Enjoying refreshments at the Hastings High School senior prom in 1961 are, from left to right, Margaret Manford, David Pacetti, unidentified, Tedra Hardin, and Leighton Middleton. (Nancy Towns.)

The Hastings High School senior prom king and queen and their court are pictured in spring of 1961. From left to right are Jo-Ann Sweat, Marsha Masters, queen Brenda Rogers, king Donnie Solano, Rosanne Sinnott, and Mary Ann Horn. (Nancy Towns.)

Jonnie Googe Padgett, a Hastings High School teacher and librarian for 36 years, is well remembered by many former students. In a poem written by Junior Tomlinson and read at the junior-senior banquet in 1946, he says of Padgett, "That good sweet lady, as she is called, is loved by many and liked by all." (Nancy Towns.)

Thelma Griffin Padgett Trent, shown here in the fall of 1967, was the Hastings High School secretary for over 20 years. (Nancy Towns.)

Participants in the Miss Hastings High School contest are pictured in 1960. From left to right are Mary Ann Horn, Patsy Brantley, Amy Ray Beach, Carole Johnson, Mary Jo Beck, Dorothy Carmean, Gretchen Knorr, Bonnie Brown, Sharon McCullar, Sandra Cornelison, Michelle West, Charlotte Frances Mickler, Louise Johns, Jackie McCullar, and Jo-Ann Sweat.

The staff members of the Hastings High School newsletter, the *Snoop*, are pictured here in the fall of 1960. They are, from left to right, (seated) Penny Greene, Marsha Masters, editor Mary Jo Beck, Dorothy Carmean, Sharon McCullar, and Mary Ellen Masters; (standing) Mary Alice Arnold, Frances Parish, Rex Knorr, and Bonnie Brown. (Nancy Towns.)

Riding the Hastings High School homecoming parade sophomore float, "Burn 'Em at the Stake," in the fall of 1962 were Jean Deese, Jedfry Carlton, Charlie Stevens, Judy Hedrick, and Bobby Cain.

The Hastings High School cheerleaders shown here at the homecoming celebration in fall 1961 are (from left to right) Michelle West, captain Sylvia Bailey, Linda Lands, cocaptain Sylvia Masters, Carolyn Edminster, and Mary Alice Arnold. (Nancy Towns.)

The Hastings High School homecoming queen and court in the fall of 1961 included Brenda Sweat, Mary Ellen Masters, Charlie Weigel, queen Sharon McCullar, king William Reynolds, Tedra Hardin, Frances Johns, and crown-bearers Brenda Wells and Mike Reynolds.

Seven

SPORTS

Sports have always been part of the lifeblood of the Hastings community. The abundant wildlife in and around the river, swamps, and forests made outdoor activities like hunting and fishing quite popular. But when it came to sports, football was king. Because of the town's competitive spirit, special "weight training," and eventually, great coaching, the Hastings Spudsters had many memorable football teams from the 1940s to the early 1960s.

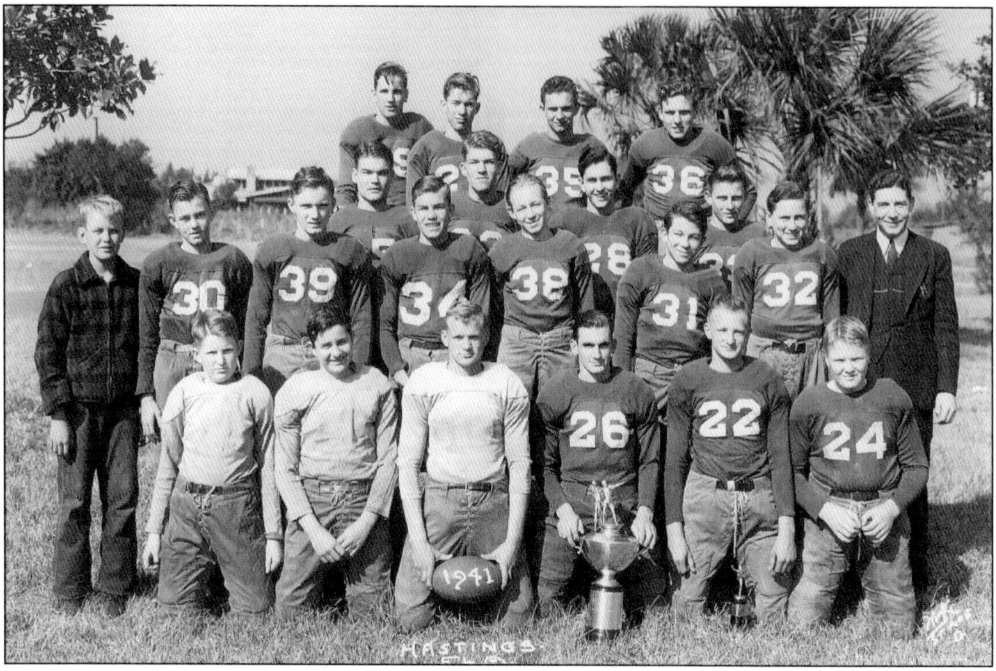

The Hastings Spudsters football team of 1941 is shown here; the team included, from left to right, (first row) Billy Flewellen, Eugene Miles, Bill Browning, Fred Kaiser, Millard "Pop" Browning, and Richard "Dick" Kelly; (second row) Glen Wallace, Tommy "Junior" Tomlinson, Harold Stevens, Bob Brough, Gerald Allen, Jimmy Freeman, Harold "Sonny" Barry, and Coach Scarborough; (third row) Russell Godwin, Warren Godwin, Bobby Miles, and Walter "Dutch" Weigel; (fourth row) George Miller, Lee Maltby, Harold Smyly, and Padgett "Pete" Miller. (Nancy Towns.)

Because Hastings was a small school, boys were drafted in the seventh grade to play football. Tommy Tomlinson (left) remembers an experience he had in study hall in seventh grade. One day, two of the biggest senior boys came by to talk to him about football. They asked if Tomlinson planned to join the team, but he said his mother would not let him. The senior boys simply responded, "Practice starts at three."

This is a photograph of the 1946 football team with No. 21 Tommy "Junior" Tomlinson in the center of the front row. In the early years, there were no weights for the football players to train with, but the boys worked after school and on weekends loading potatoes. Their weight training became lifting 100-pound bags of potatoes onto trucks and then from trucks onto railroad cars. (Chris Stanton.)

The 1946–1947 team featured seven all-conference players, including (from left to right) Glen Wallace, Charles Burrell, Tommy "Junior" Tomlinson, Donny Wilson, Billy Wilson, Benny Maltby, and Hugh Shiver.

The cheerleaders were a big part of the excitement for the Hastings Spudsters 1961 conference championship team. They could always be counted on to keep the energy, enthusiasm, and school spirit high. Pictured from left to right are Jane Lee, cocaptain Mary Jo Beck, Gretchen Knorr, Dorothy Carmean, cocaptain Sharon McCullar, and Mary Anne Horn.

Football Squad

FIRST ROW: Charlie Moody, Larry Register, Ronnie Griffin, Ranny Thomas, Frank Moore, Randy Greene.

SECOND ROW: Berry Norris, Neal Turlington, Sammy Lane, Herbert Davis, Thomas Lee, Tommie Burrell.

THIRD ROW: David Barnes, Paul Kaiser, Kenneth Johns, Charlie Weigel (Captain), Skipper Hunter, Dee Kennedy.

SCHEDULE

September 15	*	x	HHS - - - - 34	Baldwin - - - - - - - - 0
September 22	*		HHS - - - - 25	Florida Military - - - - 0
September 29		x	HHS - - - - 62	Keystone - - - - - - - 0
October 6		x	HHS - - - - 28	Callahan - - - - - - - 6
October 13	*	x	HHS - - - - 75	St. Joseph - - - - - - - 0
October 20		x	HHS - - - - 41	Taylor - - - - - - - - - 0
October 27	*	x	HHS - - - - 20	Crescent City - - - - - 0
November 3		x	HHS - - - - 48	D. & B. - - - - - - - - 7
November 10	*	x	HHS - - - - 15	Bunnell - - - - - - - - 0
November 17		x	HHS - - - - 13	Father Lopez - - - - - 7

Home Games *
Conference Games x

In 1962, Hastings High School went undefeated and won the conference championship. During the football season, they beat much larger schools like those in Bunnell, Crescent City, and Baldwin. That year, quarterback Michael Thigpen and lineman Charlie Weigle were named all-conference, and Hugh Parker received honorable mention.

Coaches
MR. BRUMLEY and
MR. SKELTON

Managers
JOHNNIE BARNES
ARTHUR JOHNS
LUTHER SWEAT

Hastings Gridders Dominate All-Conference Team

By E. D. KAISER

At the annual coaches meeting of the St. Johns River Conference, held this past weekend at Baldwin, the coaches selected

son as a SJRC member. ings defeated Lopez 13-7 in final regular season game both clubs, to take the 1961 c pionship. Lopez lost a post

Kaiser Scores Three Times To Lead Hastings To 28-6 Conference Win

By E. D. KAISER

and scored in seven plays, with

punts as the first period came a close.

Hastings Spudsters Crush Taylor High By 41-0 Score

E. D. KAISER

ragged ball at t ylor High' Wildc ning. ind 0 season rec eats homecomin Kaiser, the b nes to end Sa

Hastings Defeats Lopez 13-7, Wins SJRC Crown

By E. D. KAISER

The undefeated Hastings Spud- sters by d Lopez dium Frida score. The first wins, It als Brum

who played deserve congratula-

The half ended moments later

Spudsters In 34-0 Win In Opener

Hastings Wallops FMS 25-0; Bees Host CCHS JV's Tonight

By E. D. KAISER

son.

following for special mention, Sam of driving for their

(Record photo by Charles Olson).

Hastings Spudsters Blast Crescent City Homecoming, 20-0

By E. D. KAISER

e Hastings Spudsters capped homecoming festivities with 0 win over a defensive mind- rescent City Rebel team that alert in the fumble and pass

first downs before half-time, a Barnes to Burrell pass of yards getting one of them and Burrell reverse the other, move from the Hastings 43 the CC 34. From this point, Ferrell intercepted a Barnes the way to the Spudste

Hastings Blanks Bunnell, 15-0; Moves Nearer Title

By E. D. KAISER

Over 2,000 fans, probably the largest crowd to

by Berry Norris. A pass w complete and then Burnsed bad snap. He picked it up 15 and looking for running found himself at the go where Barnes, Lee and T ton, smacked him down f two points.

Bunnell kicked off from 20 and Hastings moved d the Bunnell 26, via a Bar Burrell pass, only to have sed intercept at that point Abbott picked up one B first down, before Sheffield

Champ Spudsters Place 6 On Mythical Team; CCHS Two

By E. D. KAISER

At the annual coaches meeting of the St. Johns River Conference, held this weekend at Baldwin, the coaches selected a 25 man all-con-

Baldwin—Dub Cobb and Clayton Hill:

Crescent City—Don Brenner and Earl Colvard:

Callahan—John Sauls and Mike

Hastings Spudsters Ramble And Roll Over St. Joe 75-0

By E. D. KAISER

This football collage from the 1962 Hastings High School yearbook, the *Sebago*, highlights the achievements of the school's conference championship team. During the season, the Hastings football team outscored its opponents an astounding 361–20.

HASTINGS '66 SPUDSTERS MAKE COACH BRUMLEY'S 100th VICTORY

This year I had the greatest enjoyment of my career as a Coach--my 100th victory. I can only contribute this to my many fine athletes of Hastings High, both past and present. Their willingness and desire are what made my success possible.

There are many things that I remember that happened throughout the years----from my first victory in 1950 with only 13 boys on the squad to our 1966 team.

Times have changed but one thing remains the same--my sincere appreciation to everyone who has helped to make this goal into a reality.

Herman "Foots" Brumley was the most famous football coach in school history. For most of his nearly 20 years in Hastings, Brumley's football teams were ranked near the top of the conference. In 1966, Coach Brumley celebrated his 100th victory at Hastings High School.

St. Johns County has long been renowned for its abundant fishing and hunting. With the St. Johns River, a natural habitat for largemouth bass and other "good eating" fish, only two miles from Hastings, men and women both young and old took advantage of the sport. Here, Dorothy (left), Emma (center), and George Coe show off their freshly caught fish around 1910.

This c. 1923 photograph shows, from left to right, Isaac Brandon (in top hat and bow tie) D.W. McElveen, D.W.'s father D.F. McElveen, and an unidentified man—along with a string of fish. The city of Brandon, Florida, located near Sarasota, was named after Isaac Brandon, and this is how he dressed even when he went fishing. (Nancy Towns.)

John Hunt (right) and an unidentified man are shown standing in front of the McElveen Hardware Store in the Hughes Building with the season record catch of 44 pounds of fish, caught in a single day, in 1925. A note on the photograph says that they were caught with live bait.

Wally (left) and Buzzy DuPont, from the pioneering Federal Point DuPont family, are pictured here with a large tarpon they caught in the St. Johns River at Devil's Elbow near Palatka. Tarpon is a saltwater big game fish, but legend has it that they are found in the St. Johns River all the way to Palatka, 75 miles from the Atlantic Ocean. This big tarpon proves it.

This picture was taken at the United Methodist Church Sunday school class picnic at Fannie and D.W. McElveen's lake cabin on June 1, 1944. From left to right are Marie Flewellen, Caroline Flewellen, Fannie McElveen, Irma Smith, Miriam Ziegler, Pearl Able (with fish), Billy Maltby, and an unidentified boy. (Nancy Towns.)

Sometimes, the "big ones" people caught were not fish. This photograph shows avid outdoorsman and hardware store owner D.W. McElveen (left) with an unidentified friend and a large alligator that they "caught" at the St. Johns River. (Nancy Towns.)

Around 1940, the St. Johns County Chamber of Commerce used this photograph, titled "Hunters with their Deer," to promote outdoor sports in the area. From left to right are Bill Wiggins, J.E. Zeigler, Emmett Campbell, and D.W. McElveen. (Nancy Towns.)

The young people in the Hastings area took competition seriously even if it did not involve sports. Nearly every year, the community sent teams to the state vegetable-judging contest sponsored by the Florida Department of Agriculture. The Hastings teams always went expecting to win. This photograph from 1958 shows state vegetable-judging first-place winners Donnie Solano, Leighton Middleton, Billy Beach, and Michael Thigpen. Standing behind the team is county agent Paul Dinkins.

Wayne Smith and Kathy Forson are shown in 1966 with a potato marketing display created for the annual 4-H competition. Their entry became the winner at the county, district, and state levels and eventually was chosen to represent Florida at the national competition held in St Louis. This potato-marketing display ultimately finished a close second to the mushroom entry from Pennsylvania. (Wayne Smith.)

Some community competitions were not taken quite so seriously. This image shows a potato-peeling contest in 1965 with county agent Paul Dinkins supervising in the background.

Local farmers also competed each year to see who could grow the largest potato. The biggest ones were put on display at Elmo's Drug Store. The contest at Elmo's was a local tradition for many years. This photograph shows George Leonard with an award-winning two-and-half-pound giant Sebago potato. The largest potato ever entered was grown on the farm of G.A. Burrell and weighed two pounds and fourteen ounces.

Eight

Churches, Social Clubs, and Civic Groups

Churches have been active in the Hastings area since the 1870s. The Cartersville Church, located southeast of Hastings, was the first in the community, followed by the Mount Olive Baptist Church, which started about 1874. Charles Perry McCullar (pictured) was founder of the Mount Olive Baptist Church. The church services were initially held in McCullar's home.

St. Paul's Episcopal Church was founded at Federal Point in 1880; prior to that date, services from the Book of Common Prayer were held by William Evans and Capt. Edwin Smith, a former ship's captain. The congregation first met in an orange grove belonging to Captain Smith and then in the hall of his general store. Plans were ready in September 1880 for the building of the church edifice.

The Northern Methodist Church, pictured in 1909, was located a half mile south of downtown. It was called the Yankee or Northern Methodist Church because most of the members were from Northern states. In 1903, while plans were underway to erect a church building, a dispute arose over its location. This dispute caused a division in the congregation and the resulting formation of two groups of Methodists in Hastings.

St. Johns Methodist & Episcopal Church, shown here in 1930, replaced the Old Northern Methodist Church. The new church, located on the corner of Church and Main Streets, was still called the Yankee or Northern Methodist Church. When the two Methodist congregations in Hastings merged to form the United Methodist Church, the St. Johns church was torn down. Rev. Addyman Smith was the pastor of this church for several years.

In 1939, the two Methodist congregations merged into one church and one building. Dr. C.E. Carroll served as the first pastor of the new United Methodist Church. Before the merger, this building, dedicated in 1917, was called the First Methodist Episcopal Church South. In the 1960s, it was renamed Christ United Methodist Church. This beautiful gray stone structure still stands at the corner of Lattin and First Streets.

The United Methodist Church youth choir is shown here in 1958. Pictured are, from left to right, (first row) Shelly Burrell, Pam Smith, Debbie Fortner, Karen Burrell, Susan Burrell, Joe Beach, Charlie Burrell, Frosty Bass, Greg Maltby, and Rusty Fridy; (second row) Paula Smyly, Pam Campbell, Elizabeth Ann Stevens, Brenda Maltby, Becky Padgett, Howard Magarian, Frank Johns, Doyle Griffin, Joel Padgett, Chuck Allen, Mark Burrell, Austin Johns; Betsy Yelvington, Leader, Connie Hill, Lee Yarborough, Mabel Turney, Nancy Parish, Ella May Stevens, Helen Johns, Jerry Browning, Kent Hill, Wayne Smith, Chris Keller, and Dale Barstow.

When the Hastings First Baptist Church was first organized, a tent served as the place of worship until a storm blew it down and destroyed the piano. After that, the Masonic Hall was used as a meeting place until 1912, when the frame building shown here was erected. This building, known as the "old Baptist Church," was used until 1926. Rev. J.W. McNamara was the first pastor.

By 1927, the membership of Hastings First Baptist Church had outgrown its original building. A committee consisting of Sherman A. Minton, George V. Leonard, J.E. Wade, Monroe A. Minton, H.A. Kuter, and Dr. Benjamin L. Padgett was appointed to solicit funds for a new building. The committee raised $25,000 in cash and borrowed $20,000 to erect the building that still stands today.

Social clubs and civic groups have played a vital role in the Hastings community. Organizations like the Wednesday Club were responsible for advocating for the public library, community beautification, and important social welfare programs. Pictured are, from left to right, (first row) Mattie Bachelder, Faith Leonard, Miss Harris, Lillie Hughes, and Mrs. Taylor; (second row) Alice Stanton and Gordon, Mrs. Smith, Nannie Gladney, Miss Moragne, Emma Coe, Atala Burchard, and Emma Brown.

The Wednesday Club was also called the Get Together and Work Club (GTWC). The GTWC members shown here in 1916 include, from left to right, (first row) Mary Catherine Middleton, Wesley Taylor, Hugh Cavanaugh, Mildred Hughes; (second row) two unidentified women, Imogene Middleton, Mrs. Taylor, Lottie Fox, and Mattie Bachelder; (third row) unidentified, Emma Coe, Atalia Burchard, unidentified, Elizabeth Proctor, unidentified, Lillie Brown Hughes, and unidentified. (Nancy Towns.)

Many lasting friendships have been formed in Hastings over the years. One group of nine girls became friends in elementary school in 1920, and their friendship lasted for more than 80 years. Nicknamed the "Nifty Nine Gang," the members were, from left to right, Ruth Campbell, Margaret Beck, Rachel Curtis, Netha Campbell, Martha Middleton, Clarice Johnson, Dorothy Yelvington, Frances McElveen, and Jean Bowles. The Nifty Nine's social activities were often reported in the *Hastings Herald*. For example, the October 25, 1929, edition of the *Herald* ran the following mention of a Nifty Nine slumber party: "Miss Christine McClinton honored the Nifty Nine Gang with a slumber-less party Saturday night. The Nine enjoyed a midnight stroll followed by a hot game of bridge and other games. Music was rendered by Dick McElveen's portable Victrola and fruits and homemade candy were served throughout the sojourn." (Nancy Towns.)

Hastings Rotary Club members are shown around 1925 in front of the original community "Town Hall." Pictured are, from left to right, (first row) unidentified, Ray Hillier, Tom Miles, three unidentified men, George W. Waller, unidentified, Graham Lee, Theron "Hank" Hall, and Don Hanna; (second row) Clarve Bachelder, Sherman Minton, Ralph Atkinson, James "Jim" Abbott, Don Barstow Sr., G. Walter Proctor, Henry Herbert "Hub" Bailey, Frederick "Fred" Kaiser Jr., Dr. Elbert Coe, Audrey Miller, and Lee Braswell.

This photograph shows the interior of the old town hall building and members of the Hastings Rotary Club about 1930. Pictured are (left to right) Don Hanna, unidentified, Sherman Minton, unidentified, Graham Lee, unidentified, Ralph Atkinson, Dr. Elbert Coe, three unidentified men, George Waller, James "Jim" Abbott, Audrey Miller, Lee Braswell, Tommy Hall, unidentified, Elmo "Buddy" DuPont, two unidentified men, and Henry Herbert "Hub" Bailey.

The Hastings Town Council shown here in 1940 included, from left to right, E. Samuel Miles, Ansley Hall, Sr., Dr. J. Lance Freeman, Harry Pellicer, Robert "Bob" Lovett, Alvin "Al" Wilke, Kenneth Bailey, Town Clerk, Barnes West, and Amos N. Wyllys. Lovett served as mayor of Hastings and was eventually elected to the board of the St. Johns County Commission. (Nancy Towns.)

The Hastings Rotary Club promotes Clean Up Week, which took place from June 22 to 28 in 1947. Pictured in front of the Hastings Civic Center are, from left to right, (first row) Dr. E.N. "Don" McCubbin, Prof. Truman Scarborough, Don Eddius, John ?, and C. Roy Sykes; (second row) Zachary "Zack" Holland, Jr., Amos Wyllys, Ross Swartzel, Dr. Elbert Coe, D.W. McElveen, Frederick "Fred" Meixner, W.A. "Billy" Hardin, Thalia Shiver, and Harry Pellicer.

This meeting of the officers of the Walker-Browning American Legion Post No. 102 took place around 1950; from left to right are unidentified, Kenneth "Kenny" Griffin, an unidentified district officer, Charles Stanton Jr., Dick Reid, Energy Cruse, William Walter "Bill" Parish, and Richard "Dick" Beck. (Nancy Towns.)

Nine

Historic Homes

The community of Elkton was originally known as Middleton. As in Hastings, the history of the development of Elkton was tied to the coming of rail service around 1890. Eventually, two trains a day stopped at Elkton, and many locals took advantage of the convenience, riding the train to St. Augustine and Palatka to sightsee or shop. The James Leighton Middleton family residence, pictured here about 1910, still stands today.

This c. 1900 photograph shows the William Dorr residence at Federal Point. Dorr came to Florida in the late 1860s, first settling at Orange Mills. Soon thereafter, he and his wife, Lydia, relocated to Federal Point and became founding members of St. Paul's Episcopal Church. William Dorr died of a bleeding stomach ulcer in Federal Point in 1908. Dr. C.A. Lattin of Hastings was his attending physician.

The Murphy family residence at Orange Mills was constructed in 1871. The farm the family developed, called Edgefield-on-the-St.-Johns, had its best year in 1925. The Great Depression was hard on the family, but they were able to keep the farm by renting the land out to tenant farmers, and Cecil M. Murphy took odd jobs before becoming a postal clerk at the East Palatka post office. (Mary Murphy.)

The railroad station agent's home in Hastings is pictured here around 1908. George and Dorothy Coe are the children sitting on the steps. On one side of the house, a small building was erected and used as Hastings's first public library. Imogene Middleton, Mae Campbell, and Dorothy Coe served as librarians for many years. (Nancy Towns.)

This building became the first schoolhouse in Hastings in 1897. The teacher was Charles DuPont. This c. 1905 photograph was taken after the building had become the residence of Dr. Elbert Coe and family. Dorothy (left), George (center), and Emma Coe—and their pet dog—are shown in their front yard. The house was later the residence of Virginia and Charnalle Campbell. (Nancy Towns.)

The George Waller family residence on Park Avenue in Hastings is pictured around 1905. Dating back to 1890, this building was the original home of Thomas Horace Hastings. The Waller Potato Company, located at one end of the Florida East Coast Railway train depot, was a prominent Hastings business until it was sold to Edgar Miles in 1931.

This c. 1905 image shows the Frank Elmer "Cap'n" Bugbee residence on Hastings Boulevard. Bugbee, an early resident, came to Hastings from Vermont via Ocala and St. Augustine. His interests eventually encompassed all facets of the potato industry.

The George Vernon Leonard family residence on Hastings Boulevard, built in 1895, is pictured here around 1915. G.V. Leonard managed the Wetumpka Fruit Company as well as several other agricultural holdings of the F.M. Leonard Company across the state of Florida.

The J. Amos Gladney and family residence on the Leonard Farm is shown here about 1906. This home was built by A.C. Carter and Gladney. The house burned to the ground in the late 1940s. (Wayne Smith.)

The Charles DuPont family residence is pictured here around 1908. Charles, the grandson of Federal Point pioneer Cornelius DuPont, moved to Hastings in 1906 and purchased this home and farm. In 1910, Charles incorporated the Hastings Development Company, serving as the company's first president and general manager selling real estate for residential development.

The George Proctor family residence is shown around 1905. George and Elizabeth Proctor moved to Hastings from Illinois around 1904 and built this brick home on the boulevard south of Hastings. Around 1914, they were joined by their nephew Russell Proctor, who married Mary Ethel Campbell, who had moved to Hastings from South Carolina with her family in 1905. The Proctor and Campbell families became prominent area farmers. (Wayne Smith.)

Ten

The Potato Capital

Hortense Miles and Irma H. Smith, the original historians of the town of Hastings, were instrumental in the placement of the first "Hastings: The Potato Capital" sign, which is shown here with Peggy Davis, the 1946 Hastings Potato Queen.

THE TOWN OF HASTINGS

In this little burg of Hastings –
It's just a country town –
Cabbage and potatoes
Supply its chief renown.
Its people are so friendly
And, in walking down the street,
There's a cheerful word of welcome
From everyone you meet.

Within two blocks on Main Street
You'll find its every store.
While it seems to be sufficient,
Some think there should be more.
Starting at the railroad
On the east side of the street
And, taking them in order,
I'll name the ones we meet.

First there's Amos Wyllys.
He runs the town Hotel.
He used to be in "groceries"
And must have done quite well.
Next is Mrs. Yelvington
In the Five and Ten Cent Store;
She'll welcome you and show you 'round
Her merchandise galore.

Then, there's Mr. Higginbotham,
Who'll tend to most your needs
Of fertilizer, feed and such
And different kinds of seeds.
And then, another Higginbotham –
"Buddy" as she's known –
She runs a first rate dry goods store
And mostly, all alone.

Now here's the town "Headquarters" –
Elmo's Sundries Store, -
Where the men all seem to congregate
And talk for evermore.
Alma runs this fine café
I think the town's in luck
To get a first class dinner
For as little as a "buck".

Here, you see Bob Lovett's,
The grocer of the town
And since he entered politics,
He's acquired some renown.

Next, you see our Beauty Shoppe;
Here like anywhere,
Our ladies spend a lot of time
A' fixin' up their hair.
And then the Children's Toggery,
Its windows are a joy
To the heart of every mother
With a little girl or boy.

Now, here is Allen's Barber Shop –
T' will never be the same –
We'll always look for Gerald,
If they ever change its name.
And I'd like to add an extra line
Of tribute, if I may:
This town was really saddened
When Gerald passed away.

And here's the local A and P.
You can look the country o'er;
Where ever there is business,
You'll find an AP store.
And this is Rhoda's Dress Shoppe.
Now, to me it would appear
What the men do down at Elmo's,
The ladies do up here.

Now comes Richard's Hardware
Where all the "fishin's" done.
An authority on everything
From a fish-hook to a gun.
And here you see the Hasting's Bank,
A noble institution,
They had some trouble some time back
That took some "restitution".

And here we come to Farm Supply,
Where the farmer thinks he's gypped,
But he can buy most anything –
They're especially equipped.
And next, the Hastings Pressing Club,
Doing well, t'would seem,
If one can gauge a business
By the exodus of steam.

And lastly Bob's Repair Shop.
His soul, it fairly bleeds
When sometimes farmers bring their gear
To alter to their needs.

Then, directly on the other side,
The biggest of them all –
Chris Stanton's place of business –
If you measure wall to wall.
Now Chris is quite a fellow;
By a few he may be cursed,
But, if I was needin' a friend,
I'd come around here first.

Jack Maltby does the lathe work
On axles, shafts and cranks;
He also works in woodwork –
His specialty is tanks.
And here, we find Farm Implement.
Young Amos runs this "show"
Under general supervision
Of Old Charlie, if you know.

Now, here's our Civic Center,
The pride of everyone;
A real credit to the town
When is said and done.
In here we keep the fire truck,
By volunteers it's manned,
Who donate of their service
With little to demand.

Next is good old Larry French
In the Western Auto Store.
You'll always find a store like this
While traveling shore to shore.
And lastly, on the corner,
A Five and Ten is found,
Stocked so full and varied
You can hardly turn around.

Now, these are all such friendly folks –
I know their woes and cares;
They're concerned about my welfare,
As I'm concerned for their's.
Now I took you on this journey
So that you could also see
That, if you lived in Hastings,
You'd feel the same as me.

H.H. SCOVILLE
– 1961 –

This poem, written by Hiram H. Scoville in 1961, charmingly and accurately describes the people and the small businesses that operated along Main Street in Hastings. (Nancy Towns.)

This 1960s aerial view of Hastings shows Hastings High School at the southern city limits and looks northward into downtown Hastings. Today, the former school building houses the Hastings Public Library and some St. Johns County offices. (Chris Stanton.)

This is another aerial view of downtown Hastings; in this case, it looks south. Note the intersection of Main Street and the old railroad line. In the foreground, on the corner north of the railroad tracks, is the Hastings Potato Growers Association building. (Chris Stanton.)

This is the "Hastings, Potato Capital of Florida" historical marker as it appears today. The marker was originally located near the downtown fire station in the civic center, but when that building was demolished, the sign was relocated to the front of the former Hastings High School, which is now the Hastings Public Library.

Bibliography

Bartram, William. *Bartram's Travels*. Philadelphia, PA: James & Johnson, 1791.

Bland & Associates, Inc., The Elkton Hastings Historic Farmstead Survey, St. Johns County, Florida. BAI Report of Investigations No. 415, prepared for St. Johns County Board of County Commissioners. Report on file, Florida Master Site File (FMSF), Division of Historical Resources, Tallahassee, FL: May 2009.

Bloomfield, Max. *Bloomfield's Illustrated Historical Guide*. St. Augustine, FL: Max Bloomfield, 1883.

Chandler, David Leon. *Henry Flagler*. New York, NY: Macmillan Publishing, 1986.

Crawford, William G., Jr. *Florida's Big Dig*. Cocoa, FL: The Florida Historical Society Press, 2006.

Gem City Booklet. *Farm and Truck Lands in The Famous Hastings Potato District*. Dayton, OH: Gem City Improvement Company, 1916.

Graham, Thomas. *Mr. Flagler's St. Augustine*. Gainesville, FL: University Press of Florida, 2014.

Hubbard, E. Stuart. *Memories of Florida*. Poughkeepsie, NY: Self-published, 1951.

Parish, Frances McElveen. "Early History of Community of Hastings," *St. Augustine Record*, February 1, 1959.

Pusey, William Allen, M.D. The Founder of Hastings, Florida. Recalled by James B. Ingraham, 1920.

Rose, G. Norman. *Irish Potato Production in Florida—A Historic Data Series*. Orlando, FL: United States Department of Agriculture, 1976.

Standiford, Les. *Last Train to Paradise*. New York: Broadway Books, 2002.

Whitney, John P. *Whitney's Florida Pathfinder*. New York: Pathfinder Books, 1876.